LEARN LIBRARY SKILLS SERIES

Learn REFERENCE WORK

Lynn Farkas
Helen Rowe

TotalRecall Publications, Inc.
1103 Middlecreek
Friendswood, Texas 77546
281-992-3131   281-482-5390 Fax
www.totalrecallpress.com

All rights reserved. Except as permitted under the United States Copyright Act of 1976, No part of this publication may be reproduced, stored in a retrieval system, or transmitted in any form or by any means electronic or mechanical or by photocopying, recording, or otherwise without prior permission of the publisher. Exclusive worldwide content publication / distribution by TotalRecall Publications, Inc.

Copyright © 2017 Lynn Farkas and Helen Rowe

ISBN: 978-1-59095-441-6
UPC: 6-43977-44416-5
Printed in the United States of America with simultaneous printing in Australia, Canada, and United Kingdom.

INTERNATIONAL EDITION
1 2 3 4 5 6 7 8 9 10

Library or Congress Control Number: 2016962699

Judgments as to the suitability of the information herein is the purchaser's responsibility. TotalRecall Publications, Inc. extends no warranties, makes no representations, and assumes no responsibility as to the accuracy or suitability of such information for application to the purchaser's intended purposes or for consequences of its use except as described herein.

The scanning, uploading and distribution of this book via the Internet or via any other means without the permission of the publisher is illegal and punishable by law. Please purchase only authorized electronic editions and do not participate in or encourage electronic piracy of copyrighted materials. Your support of the author's rights is appreciated.

TABLE OF CONTENTS

CHAPTER ONE What is Reference Work? 1
CHAPTER TWO Reference Services 9
CHAPTER THREE The Reference Interview..19
CHAPTER FOUR The Search Strategy 31
CHAPTER FIVE Introduction to Reference Tools 43
CHAPTER SIX Online Resources...59
CHAPTER SEVEN Dictionaries and Encyclopedias 71
CHAPTER EIGHT Organizational, Biographical and Trade Directories 91
CHAPTER NINE Yearbooks, Handbooks, Almanacs and Manuals 113
CHAPTER TEN Geographic Tools 121
CHAPTER ELEVEN Government Documents 131
CHAPTER TWELVE Specialized Information Sources..157
CHAPTER THIRTEEN Delivering Information 169
CHAPTER FOURTEEN Evaluating Reference Services...177
ANSWERS 185
GLOSSARY..203
BIBLIOGRAPHY...212
INDEX...214

ACKNOWLEDGEMENTS

Thanks to Mary Gosling, Clara L. Sitter and Colin Gray who wrote the previous editions of *Learn reference work*, and who kindly allowed their text to form the basis of this international edition.

Many thanks to our colleagues, family and friends who have offered their suggestions, knowledge and expertise in the updating of this publication. Thank you for your never-ending patience. We are also thankful to those students who have asked the questions to which this book provides the answers.

PREFACE

Learn reference work is an introduction to the basic knowledge and skills required to work in the reference section of a library or other information agency, at a professional or paraprofessional level. The workbook presents a foundation of theory and information for good reference service, along with additional concepts related to services and models.

Since the last edition of *Learn reference work*, the availability of more electronic resources, and of the Internet, has dramatically changed the way that reference work is conducted. To align with this shift in focus, *Learn reference work* has been comprehensively rewritten. Those familiar with previous editions of the text will note that chapters have been rearranged and content has been extensively updated and expanded. This has allowed a stronger focus on electronically available resources, including newer technologies and formats of information available to users. The increased use of Readers' Advisory has also been addressed. New chapters are included on the search strategy; online resources; government documents available in the United States, Canada and Australia; and specialized information sources such as the United Nations, intergovernmental organizations and non-governmental organizations. In spite of the rapid changes in the way that information is gathered and distributed, however, the basic goal of reference service remains constant: to connect users with information.

Although libraries use fewer printed reference sources, we have included a combination of print and electronic sources to accommodate those who may not have access to electronic versions. Print resources are included in each of the chapters as appropriate.

Learn reference work is a combination text and workbook, designed for use on its own or in a formal course of study. It is suitable for use in a classroom, and by those who are studying by themselves, either with a specific goal or as part of their continuing professional development. Throughout the book there are exercises to practice and test skills, and quizzes to test understanding. There are answers for self-checking at the back of the book. Since some of the exercises relate to individual libraries and experiences, they do not all have answers, and some answers are provided for guidance only. Users may not always agree completely with the answers given, so it would be useful to check your answers with a teacher or experienced reference staff member.

Reference materials are subject to frequent editions, revisions, and updates. Electronic resources are updated even more frequently. This creates a challenge when preparing exercises that are relevant and current. We have endeavored to provide questions that are general enough to be answered without consulting a specific title or edition. Please note that the answers provided were correct at the time of publication.

NOTE ON SPELLING AND CAPITALIZATION

This edition is designed for use in North America, Europe and Australasia, across countries that employ different spelling conventions for English words. For consistency, American spelling has been adopted for the text.

Titles included in the text are capitalized according to standard library cataloging practice—that is, apart from names, only the first word of the title has a capital letter. This is intended to accustom library students and staff to this style.

CHAPTER ONE
What is Reference Work?

Introduction
Reference work is the aspect of library work that provides assistance to users seeking information. This includes:
- individual client assistance, face-to-face or online
- meeting requests for specific information
- alerting users to new developments in their area
- research on behalf of clients
- training in the use of reference and research tools.

Purpose of Reference Work
The basic purpose of reference work is to help users find information in the library's collection, by selecting the best sources (physical and online) from that collection and referring users to other appropriate sources.

Types of Reference Work
Reference work can range from answering simple questions like the population of France to complex queries requiring specialist research skills. Specific activities performed by reference staff will be covered in Chapter Two of this book; however, all reference work deals with the following types of reference queries:

- **directional**—requiring knowledge of the physical layout of the library, e.g., "Where are the maps shelved?"
- **instructional or reader education**—educating people to use the library's resources effectively, e.g., "How do I use ProQuest?"
- **ready reference**—providing factual information from one or two simple sources, e.g., "What is the currency of China?"
- **readers' advisory**—recommending titles or authors for pleasure reading, e.g., "Can you recommend a good thriller?"
- **research**—answering complex questions requiring multiple sources, e.g., "What is the impact of current levels of unemployment on the Social Security Systems of France, the U.S. and Canada?"
- **referrals**—suggesting community agencies for services outside the library, e.g., "Where could I get a tourist map of the city?"

EXERCISE 1.1

Look at the following questions and decide the category of reference query to which they belong—i.e., directional, instructional (or reader education), ready reference, readers' advisory, research or referrals. You do not have to answer the questions, just determine the type of query.

1. I want a good introductory book on astronomy.

2. I want some information on zoology.

3. Can you suggest a good murder mystery?

4. Where are the newspapers shelved?

5. Who wrote the book *Information architecture for the World Wide Web*?

6. I require some recent articles about the value of immunizing children against measles.

7. How do I use the library catalog?

8. I need some information on the history and development of the New Zealand wool industry.

9. How do you stop a persistent cough?

10. Where do you keep the large-print fiction?

11. Where is Pokhara?

12. Where can I get legal aid advice?

13. Do you have any pictures of the Victoria Falls in Africa?

14. Please will you show me how to use the Internet? I am looking for some information on the importance of exercise.

15. Give me everything you have on Napoleon Bonaparte.

The Reference Section

Reference work varies with the purpose and size of the library. Large libraries may have a special reference section devoted to research or complex queries, with staff who deal with specific subject areas. There will often be a separate reference desk, in addition to the general circulation desk, to meet the needs of its users. Bear in mind, however, that users will usually ask for help at the first desk they see. This means that circulation staff may have to refer users to the reference desk, or handle simpler questions themselves. Academic, state and large public libraries are types of libraries that have separate reference sections and reference staff.

Smaller organizations may have only one or two staff to provide a wide variety of reference services. Smaller facilities will likely have one point of access (and one staff member) for clients to gain assistance, whether this be for reference or loan queries. Smaller public libraries and special library staff will usually juggle reference services with other library tasks.

Large or small, most libraries have a reference collection that consists of both print publications and electronic resources. The Internet has greatly increased the range of resources available for finding information and answering questions. As a consequence, there is less reliance on the print format since more information is available electronically and accessed online. Since electronic resources are available 24/7, clients are no longer limited to accessing reference resources only when the physical library is open.

In summary:
- the purpose of every library is to connect users with information
- reference services help users to make the best use of library resources
- reference work involves helping users find information quickly and efficiently through internal reference collections or external sources
- reference work may be done by staff in special reference sections in larger libraries, or as part of the general duties of staff members in smaller libraries.

Reference Staff

The reference desk is often seen as the hub of the library. Many clients seek reference help before attempting to look in a catalog. Since the purpose of a library is to serve the needs of its clients, working on the reference desk is often challenging and interesting.

Reference staff should be approachable. Behaviors contributing to an approachable appearance include making eye contact, smiling, giving a friendly greeting, and giving full attention to each question. Once the user approaches staff, other behaviors include showing interest, listening, searching, and following up. These behaviors are discussed more fully in the document *Guidelines for behavioral performance of reference and information service providers* (http://www.ala.org/rusa/resources/guidelines/guidelinesbehavioral), prepared by the Reference and User Services Association, a division of the American Library Association.

Reference staff should be proactive as well as reactive. In addition to dealing with users familiar with the library, they should watch for those who are too timid to approach library staff at a desk or who are uncertain of where to go or what to do in the library. Libraries often schedule 'roving' librarians to move through the facility actively looking for ways to be helpful to these tentative users.

All reference staff should familiarise themselves with library procedures and policies, such as registrations, emergencies, telephone procedures, dealing with difficult clients, etc. Reader education and training, such as instruction in how to use the catalog, may also be the task of the reference staff so it is important to practice these skills.

It is an advantage if library staff are familiar with local and current affairs, as requests may be linked to news items. Reading the newspaper, checking community notices and listening to local radio and television news can help with general local knowledge. Newsfeeds from various authoritative Internet news sites (eg BBC, CNN, ABC) can assist in keeping up to date with national and international news.

Never assume knowledge. If you do not know an answer, refer the client to others who might be able to help. Be prepared to call for help in busy times—pride in coping has no place in a busy reference section, especially if it means that clients wait, or leave without help.

Characteristics of Reference Staff

Staff working in reference services must develop skills in accessing information and assisting users. They need to know the library's collection and understand how to find information efficiently.

Personal Characteristics

When providing reference services, you need to be:
- tactful
- tenacious in searching for answers
- approachable
- enthusiastic about reference work.

You should also have:
- a good general knowledge
- an analytical mind
- an interest in finding information
- a commitment to delivering high quality customer service.

Communication Skills
You need:
- active listening skills
- appropriate questioning techniques
- the ability to give instructions and explain procedures
- positive body language
- the ability to put people at ease
- skills working with all ages and temperaments.

Knowledge Base
You must know:
- the collection, particularly the reference collection
- how to formulate a search strategy and practice good search techniques
- library policies and rules
- when to refer the inquiry to another library or information agency
- the principles of good customer service
- how to conduct a reference interview.

Ethics
Library staff follow a code of ethics which outlines that they should always:
- remain objective
- provide the right information
- avoid making judgements about the clients or the questions asked
- avoid interpreting the information
- avoid giving legal, medical or financial advice
- respect the confidentiality of each query
- provide equal service to all
- remember legal implications when supplying information.

Although you should try to treat all library clients equally, some libraries prepare guidelines on the level of service provided to various types of clients. For example, research staff in an academic library are likely to receive more assistance than undergraduate students.

In more than sixty countries, library associations have developed and approved national codes of professional conduct that all reference staff should keep in mind. These codes of ethics can be found at http://www.ifla.org/faife/professional-codes-of-ethics-for-librarians.

 **Activity 1.2**
Find the website for a library association in your country. Does it have a code of ethics for its members? How well does the code cover the points noted above?

Pressures at the Reference Desk

Working in a reference area can be demanding and may require facing the following situations:

- managing several questions at once
- adjusting to an irregular pace of questions
- balancing telephone or virtual requests with face-to-face requests
- coping with demanding patrons
- dealing with interruptions.

In busy and understaffed libraries, pressures can bring about exhaustion and frustration that may ultimately lead to poor service. Consequently, busy libraries may limit reference shifts to two or three hours at a time.

Coping with Demanding Patrons

The way you communicate with library users is always important, but becomes critical when dealing with difficult or angry patrons. What you say (and don't say) and how you say it will set the tone for the ensuing conversation.

It is important for the reference section to have policies and procedures for dealing with difficult patrons. These should ideally be written documents, and include information on appropriate language to use and actions to be taken. The policies should be reviewed regularly to keep them up-to-date, and all staff should be trained in the recommended procedures.

When challenging situations occur consider the following guidelines:

1. Use positive language and speak in a relaxed and low tone.

2. Develop communication skills. Listen carefully to the user's question, request, or complaint and remain calm and receptive.

3. Remain polite and professional and avoid humor or personal remarks.

4. Always observe the verbal and nonverbal messages of your users and respond accordingly.

5. Paraphrase what the user says in order to be sure you understand their comments.
6. Keep the conversation focused. Stick to the issue and do not get sidetracked by new complaints or arguments.
7. Refer to policies. If you don't think an exception should be made, explain the policy and give an explanation of its rationale. Try to offer a choice of alternatives that do not violate policy.
8. Refer to a supervisor when necessary.

When speaking with a difficult patron, remember to remain calm and focused on the issue, offering solutions whenever possible. Avoid using negative language by rephrasing your responses to make them positive. The following examples may assist:

Instead of	Say
That's not my job.	I'm not authorized to do that, but I'll find someone who can.
That's not handled by my department.	Let me find out who deals with that area.
We've always done it this way.	That's our current policy, but I'll ask our director if it could be reconsidered.
That's not available.	It's not in right now. I can put a reserve on it or check if it's available in another library.
I don't know.	I don't know, but I'll find out for you.
You need to go to the circulation desk for more help.	Let me take you over to the circulation desk, where we can get more information on that item.
You need to take your child home.	For your child's safety, we have a firm policy that children must be accompanied by an adult.

Adapted from *Dealing with difficult patrons.* Presented by Tricia Richards, The PR Dept., LLC http://www.ineedprhelp.com

You cannot always tell which interactions with patrons are going to be positive and those that will be negative, but your reaction to any situation is within your control. It is essential, therefore, for you to remain calm and to maintain the dignity of both the patron and yourself. Always aim to provide a positive experience for everyone who visits the library.

 **ACTIVITY 1.3**

Consider the following scenarios. Using the examples shown above, how would you respond to the library patron?

Case Study 1

Riccardo is a member of the public visiting a joint use library. He wishes to borrow one of the textbooks for his private study. Susan explains that in this library textbooks can only be borrowed by the students studying that subject. Riccardo is annoyed and loudly demands that since the book is available he has as much right to access the book as any of the students.

Case Study 2

Magda has watched all the DVDs in a series except the newest one. She has checked the catalog and not been able to find it listed even though she requested that the library buy the new DVD some time ago. Magda becomes very agitated, accuses the library of not ordering the DVD and insists on speaking to someone who can tell her the status of her request.

Case Study 3

Two small children are running around in the children's section of the library. Their mothers are sitting in another area of the library and are busy in conversation. As the mothers don't seem to be aware of their children's behavior, you ask the children to calm down, yet their noisy behavior continues.

CHAPTER TWO
Reference Services

Introduction
Reference services provided by library staff should always be based on the needs of the client group. Services can deal with questions, collections and other user needs. The following are some of the main forms of reference services:

Question-based services
- library assistance
- answers to questions
- readers' advisory

Collection-based services
- reference collection
- collection development
- equipment access

Extended services
- library instruction
- literature searches
- finding tools and websites
- promotion and marketing
- current awareness.

Question-based Services
Library Assistance
Many library patrons need assistance using the library, particularly the first time they visit. They often need help searching the catalog, locating material on the shelves, or finding information in reference sources. Some people feel comfortable using a library, but are unfamiliar with electronic sources and may request help using electronic databases or the Internet. Reference staff give advice on search techniques and explain how to use the library's resources.

Answers to Questions
A number of people come to a library to find the answer to a particular question or information need. They ask for help at the reference desk (this may be in the physical library setting or the virtual library environment) because they are unsure where to start searching.

The questions range from apparently simple questions—e.g., "Where are the cookbooks?"—to complex research topics such as "What effect did missionaries have on the political development of Africa?" Reference staff are trained to find answers to questions, help users find needed information, and assist clients at all levels of information seeking. Some libraries have policies and procedures about how much assistance can be provided—e.g., school library staff may help students search for information but not directly answer their assignment questions.

Readers' Advisory
Library users often come to the library looking for recreational reading. A readers' advisor is a library staff member who advises readers on their choice of books. Generally only the largest libraries have a separate desk and staff for readers' advisory services. It is more common for reference staff to assume this responsibility as well as providing information services. Most North American public libraries offer some sort of readers' advisory service, and it is becoming increasingly popular in other countries and other types of libraries.

Collection-based Services
Reference Collection
Perhaps the most important part of a reference section is its collection of resources. The *reference collection* consists of works to help users find information or refer them to other sources of information. Printed reference sources are usually shelved close to the reference desk for convenience and so that the reference staff can assist users. Many reference sources are now available in electronic form as well as in print. The reference staff aid patrons in using these sources efficiently. A small select group of frequently used resources at the reference desk is sometimes called the *ready reference* collection (discussed more fully in Chapter Five).

Collection Development
Although most libraries regard acquisition work as part of the technical services of the library, reference staff play a role in selecting material for the reference collection and at times for the library collection in general. They consistently monitor the reference collection to ensure its print and electronic resources are relevant and up-to-date. They keep abreast of new reference tools and evaluate their usefulness. They may work closely with acquisitions staff by recommending material for purchase.

Continual evaluation of the strengths and weaknesses of the library's collection is an important part of the selection process. Since part of the role of reference staff is in helping users find information from the library's general collections, these staff are well placed to recommend material for the general collection as well. Collection selection is an important task as it helps staff develop a depth of knowledge of sources the library holds, thus increasing their effectiveness in providing reference services.

Equipment Access
An additional reference 'service' deals not with information, but with providing appropriate technology for users. Photocopiers are generally available to enable users to copy relevant information. Most libraries provide free wi-fi, computing facilities, and access to printers, scanners and email to assist users in preparing reports or recording data. Libraries may circulate other equipment such as laptop computers, or e-readers to complement e-book collections. Reference staff often supervise the provision and maintenance of these services.

Extended Services

Library Instruction

Reference staff provide education on library use to individuals and groups of users. Instruction may be formal or informal, mediated or non-mediated, taking a number of forms:
- orientation tours for new users that provide a general overview of the layout of the library, location of the different collections, library procedures, etc.
- training sessions on how to use specific resources or overviews of special collections
- guides to collections and services, in print or electronic form
- programs to develop users' skills in finding, retrieving, analyzing and using information.

The first three of these forms are referred to as *reader education* services; the final one as *information literacy education*. Both types of services may be delivered in the library, in an external space, or as online tutorials. The latter is increasing in importance as more and more library clients do not use the physical library space but only access library resources online.

Literature Searches

When a library user has a complex research question, reference staff will look for relevant information within the library's collection and also search online databases, electronic resources or Internet websites. Some libraries encourage users to do their own searches, or to request a research consultation with an appropriate subject specialist who can advise them of the time and resources that may be involved.

Reference staff in academic and special libraries conduct literature searches for academics and research staff and often create an annotated bibliography to disseminate the most relevant resources. In some cases, the reference staff may prepare a literature review that analyzes and synthesizes the relevant resources.

Literature searches can be a major component of reference work in many libraries. There are a number of articles that deal with how to do literature searches and create bibliographies and literature reviews, including Lori Havard's clear and simple overview titled *How to conduct an effective and valid literature search*, which is available at http://www.nursingtimes.net/nursing-practice/clinical-zones/educators/how-to-conduct-an-effective-and-valid-literature-search/217252.article.

Finding Tools and Websites

Many libraries publish library guides or pamphlets on their collections and services. These may incorporate a map of the library highlighting various collections and service points. Libraries also publish subject guides and pathfinders on specific subjects. Here relevant resources are grouped by sub-topics or format in order to facilitate the client's access to information. These are usually web based and are linked to the library's webpage.

Most libraries maintain their own websites, or library pages on their parent organization's website. These are invaluable tools for accessing the library's collections, and are also a means to provide remote reference services for online users.

Promotion and Marketing
It is important for the library to promote its services to current and potential clients, so that the library is regularly used and its value is appreciated. Reference staff, as the 'public' face of the library, are front-line promotors and marketers of library services. The reference services listed above are useful methods of promoting the services that the library provides.

Current Awareness
Current awareness services ensure that library users keep up-to-date with information in their interest or subject areas. This information is distributed in various ways including email, social media, library's newsletter and library's website. Services may include:

- **alert services**—email notifications are automatically sent for new citations from selected databases (usually of journal articles or book tables of contents) that match a client's interests.
- **bibliographies or reading lists**—lists of works on a particular topic of interest (also called pathfinders) are prepared for users. These are usually created as annotated bibliographies that not only provide a full citation of the item, location and access, but also include a description of the content and its relevance to the topic.
- **bulletins and newsletters**—print or electronic bulletins or newsletters may be prepared and distributed with news about the library, details of new services, lists of newly acquired resources, and other items likely to be of interest.
- **displays**—new additions to the library are displayed in a prominent position, or exhibits on a particular subject are prepared. New titles may also be 'advertised' on the library's homepage.
- **journal circulation**—new issues of journals are sent to users who have expressed an interest in reading them.
- **journal title and contents page**—contents pages are sent to users on request.
- **lists of Internet sites**—Internet sites relevant to users' interests are highlighted or bookmarked for the users.
- **media monitoring**—articles are copied from print or online newspapers, websites, broadcasts, etc. and sent to users as requested. Commercial monitoring companies may be contracted to provide these services to the library and its clients.
- **new titles lists**—a list of resources recently added to the collection is prepared and distributed to users or made available via email or the Internet. These are often automatically generated within the library management system against a pre-set client profile.
- **RSS feeds**—new material on websites, blogs, etc. is sent directly to clients whenever the site is updated. Libraries often combine the information taken from multiple RSS feeds and disseminate it to clients.
- **selective dissemination of information (SDI)**— clients are asked about their information needs and supplied with items to fit those needs as the library receives them. This service is usually provided by special and academic libraries and involves a preliminary interview with the client to establish an exact profile of the information required. This profile may be fine-tuned as the client provides feedback on the relevance of the information the library retrieves.
- **social media**—Facebook pages, Twitter feeds, blogs, YouTube sites and other forms of social media are used to keep clients aware of developments in the library.

ACTIVITY 2.1

Visit a library and find out what services are offered. Complete the following table based on information gathered from guides, websites, handouts and observations.

Service	Offered? (Y/N)
Assistance in using the library	
Answers to questions	
Readers' advisory	
Reference collection - print	
Reference collection - electronic	
Collection development	
Equipment access	
Literature searches	
Orientation tours	
Reader education services	
Information literacy education	
Alert services	
Bibliographies or reading lists	
Bulletins and newsletters	
Displays	
Journal circulation	
Journal titles and contents lists	
Lists of Internet sites	
Media monitoring	
New titles lists	
RSS feeds	
Selective dissemination of information	
Social media	
Finding tools and websites	
Promotion and marketing	

Models of Reference Services

There are many ways a library can structure its reference service. Cassell provides a summary in the following table:

Type	Description	Pros	Cons
Traditional reference desk	Librarian serves user at the reference desk	Easy to staff—one service point	Only serves users who come to the desk
Reference consultation model	Complex questions are referred to a consultation service	Uses librarians for complex questions	Limits the number of users that can be served
Tiered reference service	Three levels of service—information desk, general reference desk, and consultation service	Users consult librarians for complex questions	Must train staff to do appropriate referrals and limits the number of users that can be served
Team staffing	Reference staff work together at reference desk	Librarian available to answer more difficult questions	Other library staff must make appropriate referrals to the librarian
Integrated service point concept	Integration of reference and circulation desks	Only one point of service for users	Requires ongoing training of staff
Roving	Reference staff circulate throughout the reference area	Reach users who have not approached the reference desk	May require additional staffing
Virtual reference	Reference staff answer questions by email, chat, SMS, etc.	Users assisted who cannot visit the library	Technology still needs improvement
Outreach model	Reference staff reach out to departments, groups and organizations	Can reach new audiences	May require additional staffing
Reverse-tier service model	Reference staff work within classes and organizations as the first step in providing reference service	Users can get answers for 'at the moment' questions	Requires more staff to provide this service
No reference desk	Users can make an appointment with reference staff or contact them by telephone, email, chat or SMS	More flexibility for reference staff and users	May be confusing for users who expect a reference desk

Cassell, K. A. & Hiremath, U. (2011). *Reference and information services in the 21st century: an introduction*. New York: Neal Schuman. Second revised edition. p. 424

The traditional model for providing reference service is the reference desk. Some busy libraries provide a tiered service or differentiated services to make the best use of the reference librarian. Libraries offering a tiered service often provide an information desk where directional questions are answered. Routine reference questions are directed to the traditional reference desk, and research questions may be handled by appointment. The differentiated services model expands the tiered concept to include technical assistance and instructional services.

Differentiated services help to avoid a bottleneck at a busy reference desk. Many users will not wait at a reference desk for more than a few minutes. Libraries can anticipate peak times and staff accordingly, or have support available to call when there is a rush.

Most reference departments provide some level of differentiated services. The advantages of this are:
- directions or general information can be provided by support staff
- technical assistance is best provided by 'roving' staff available to respond to users positioned at workstations
- reference questions can be addressed at the traditional reference desk
- research questions or consultation require longer encounters and can be handled by 'on call' librarians or by appointment
- instruction and reader education can be handled in a variety of ways.

Telephone reference services have been available in most libraries for many years. However, technology has expanded the options for providing services to external, remote or online users. Now, larger library systems may provide telephone reference through call centers, allowing smaller branches to focus on readers' advisory services. Email, online chat, *Ask a Librarian* and social media are virtual options that can provide a 24/7 reference service.

16 LEARN REFERENCE WORK

EXERCISE 2.2

What model of reference service is encountered in each of the scenarios described below? (There may be more than one answer for some of these scenarios.)

1. Jane comes into the library and asks a reference question. The person she speaks to contacts the science librarian who will assist Jane.

2. While Anne is borrowing resources from the library she asks where she might find further information about spectroscopy.

3. Hasan is studying late at night and sends a question to the library using the *Ask a Librarian* facility.

4. Raphael rings the reference contact number to arrange an appointment to discuss his reference query.

5. The reference librarian has an office within the Education Department where she is available to assist with research.

6. While Lina is browsing through the reference collection the reference librarian approaches her to ask if she needs assistance.

7. Luis takes queries electronically, then provides ready reference answers and access to databases.

8. Nada works at the reference desk and is available for any clients who require assistance.

9. James provides answers to directional and simple questions but refers more complex queries to the reference librarian.

10. The reference librarian provides students with specialist research support through scheduled workshops.

Factors Impacting Service

While libraries strive to offer the best, most comprehensive services to their clients, there are often factors that limit what can reasonably be provided. Factors influencing the reference services offered include:

Facility—e.g., the range of reference or research services offered may be determined by
- type of library (public vs special)
- function or mission
- technology available

Collection—e.g., a small number of reference tools can limit direct services and require more referrals to other sources
- collection size
- scope
- budget allocation

Staff—e.g., the number of staff available can affect the amount of assistance offered to users
- workloads
- expertise
- staff training

Clients—e.g., researchers or scholars require different services to large numbers of schoolchildren
- needs
- numbers

REVISION QUIZ 2.3

Use the following questions to revise your understanding of reference services. You do not need to write down the answers.

1. What is a ready reference collection?

2. What role does a Readers' Advisor play in a reference area?

3. Name three current awareness services provided by libraries.

4. Match the following models of reference service to their description:

Model of service	Description
1. Virtual reference	A. Enables reference staff to talk with users who do not approach the reference desk
2. Outreach model	B. All staff in the reference section work together on the reference desk
3. Roving	C. Reference staff visit users where they are in an office or department
4. Team staffing	D. Reference staff answer questions electronically

5. Describe two factors that might impact on the provision of a reference service.

CHAPTER THREE
The Reference Interview

Introduction

One of the most challenging aspects of reference work is communicating with library users. Communication may take place in a face-to-face meeting in the library, on the telephone, or electronically using virtual communication tools such as email, chat services, instant messaging, texting, twitter, skype or video conferencing. Regardless of the communication method, reference staff use the same skills in order to provide answers and assistance to their users.

Some information seekers have a difficult time articulating their questions, and may give unclear indications of their requirements. Sometimes several exchanges can take place between the reference staff member and the library user to identify the unexpressed information needs.

The conversation that a reference staff member has with a user to determine information needs is referred to as the *reference interview*. It is a communication process.

 A reference interview is the face-to-face, telephone or electronic exchange between a reference staff member and user to communicate, refine or clarify a reference query.

Purpose of the Reference Interview

Library staff conduct a reference interview in order to:
- determine the information needs of the client
- assist the client to locate the required information in a timely manner
- enable the library staff to assess the client's library skills
- explain the library's resources and services if required.

During the reference interview reference staff may need to encourage the client by asking questions and rephrasing statements in order to find out exactly what is being asked. By spending time checking the information need, staff avoid wasting time seeking the wrong information, and ensure that they are on track to meet the client's needs.

The Steps in a Reference Interview

In order to conduct an effective reference interview, whether in a face-to-face situation or by telephone or online, first questions should address: *who?, what?, when?, where?, why?,* and *how?*.
- **Who** will use this information? What is the user's educational ability?
- **What** format does this information need to take? **What** is the subject?
- **When** is it needed? Are there time restrictions?

- **Where** should this information come from? Is there a relevant geographic location?
- **Why** is it needed? What will it be used for?
- **How** is the search to be conducted? That is, are there any restrictions?

Following the steps outlined below will assist you in undertaking an effective reference interview.

1. **Find out** what information the client requires. The client might explain what he or she wants, but many clients use an indirect approach—e.g., they ask whether the library holds copies of *National Geographic*, but they actually want information about Mount Kilimanjaro.
2. **Ask** the client to clarify the topic. You must avoid misunderstandings that could occur due to the way the question is interpreted.
3. **Repeat** or paraphrase the question to ensure you understand what information is being sought.
4. **Find out** what the client already knows and what sources (if any) have been consulted. It can be useful to know why the client needs the information, but you will need to ask tactfully and not invade his or her privacy. Be aware that some clients will be reluctant to tell you why they want the information.
5. **Check** how soon the information is needed, and therefore how much time is available to answer the question.
6. **Develop a search strategy** to find the required information quickly and efficiently. This is often done in close consultation with the client. If you have conducted a successful reference interview, you should be thinking about relevant sources. If you cannot think of a source, start with an encyclopedia, which often leads to other sources. Consulting other library staff may also lead to suitable sources. (See Chapter Four for a more detailed discussion of search strategies.)

Conducting the Interview
Be Approachable
Many clients start a conversation with "This probably sounds like a silly question but..." Staff must reassure the client that all queries are of value and that the library is there to serve his or her needs.

Some clients find libraries confusing and intimidating. They may consider their question is not worthwhile or they may be reluctant to bother library staff. It is important, therefore, that staff make clients feel welcome and at ease. The initial verbal and non-verbal responses of staff will influence the level of interaction between the library and clients.

In order to help the client feel at ease:
- make eye contact even when you are busy—eye contact can assure clients you are aware they are waiting for help
- smile
- be prepared to help—stop the work you are doing
- use a friendly tone of voice
- stand up and move—don't just point in the general direction of the shelves or the computers but take the client to the relevant area

- appear confident—take time to consider the query and develop a search strategy based on your knowledge of the reference tools and the general collection
- be patient and courteous even with difficult clients.

Show Interest

Although some reference queries may not appear interesting to you, remember the topic is of interest to the client. Aim to provide a good reference service regardless of your personal interests.

Your interest in the client's request can be demonstrated by maintaining eye contact, making attentive comments, giving the client your full attention, and appearing unhurried.

Communicate Positively

It is extremely important to listen carefully to ensure you completely understand the client's qustion. When necessary ask appropriate questions to clarify the request.

Be courteous and don't interrupt the client while they explain their information need. It is a good idea to paraphrase or summarize the question in order to make sure you understand what is required, and to verify the question before searching. Avoid using jargon when talking to your clients as library terminology may not be understood by the person you are assisting.

Questioning the Client

Phrase your questions carefully in order to determine the client's needs quickly and efficiently.

The most effective type of question is an *open-ended question*, which allows clients to explain everything they know about the topic, and to describe their information need as clearly as possible. For example:
- Can you tell me more about what you need?
- What type of information are you looking for?
- We have a number of books about your topic. Could you give me more specific details?
- I am not sure I understand what your question means. Can you give me some more information?
- How will you use this information?

On the other hand, *closed questions* give clients the option of answering 'yes' or 'no' or selecting between several options. For example:
- Do you need journal articles?
- Are you after historical information?
- Do you want a bibliography on ancient civilizations?

You should use closed questions—e.g., "Is this information recent enough?"—only after clients have had the opportunity to explain their request.

22   LEARN REFERENCE WORK

Readers' Advisory Interviews

Readers' advisory conversations with users are more informal and personal than the informational interview, but the same interviewing and questioning processes apply. The aim of a readers' advisory interview is to determine both the interests and complexity levels of the client—for example, do they enjoy simple stories, or those with intricate plots? Personal tastes vary, so one person's 'good book' may not be appreciated by someone else. It is safe to prefer descriptive, factual statements such as 'award-winning' or 'fast-paced', to subjective statements. Suggesting, rather than recommending, titles puts the readers' advisory librarian in a more professional relationship with the user and is advised in most situations.

ACTIVITY 3.1

For further information on the reference interview, read Module 2 of 'ORE on the Web' *by Ohio Library Council* http://www.olc.org/ore/2interview.htm. *Complete the exercises located within the module.*

Communication Problems

Library clients often have difficulty explaining their needs and may need to be encouraged to provide further information.

Client	Reference Staff
Will often ask a very vague or broad question.	Ask open-ended questions to obtain more information.
May mumble so that you have difficulty understanding what they say.	Repeat what you think they said or ask them to repeat the question.
Assume that because you work in a library you know the answer to everything, including every detail of the resources in the collection.	This is impossible, but make sure you keep up-to-date with additions to the collection.
Often ask for information on behalf of someone else, which may mean they have incomplete details.	You need as much information as possible or you may have to persuade the client to go and find out more detail then return to the library.

Virtual reference exchanges require many of the same skills as face-to-face inquiries, but the nature of the virtual environment also requires skilful use of technology. For example, when using chat facilities you may encounter the following differences:

Virtual	Face-to-face
Communicating can be complex. Typing is slower than speaking.	Communicating is direct. The patron sees and hears you.
There are no visual cues to give you information about the patron or the patron's response to your comments.	Visual cues give you additional information.
Silence is not okay as the user can't see what you are doing for them.	Silence is okay if the patron can see what you're doing.
Queuing requires extra steps, requiring that users be informed of wait times.	Queuing for assistance is based on seeing other users waiting.
Reference staff member needs to be proactive in following-up on transactions, knowing when to place the responsibility of follow-up back on the patron.	Responsibility for follow-up can be transferred to the patron.
Multitasking is required for conversation, typing, and sending while searching or waiting for the patron's response.	Process is sequential as you go through the reference interview process.
You may not be serving your primary clientele.	You are serving your primary clientele.

Regardless of the environment in which the reference interview is conducted, if the communication channels are not clear the client may receive wrong or misleading information. The library staff and the client will then waste time, and the client may become frustrated with the library and its services.

Follow-Up

The final part of the reference process is to determine whether the client is satisfied with the answer provided. In most cases you will be able to find an answer to a question, but you should ensure the answer fully satisfies the client. If the answer is not satisfactory, you may need to refer the client to another member of staff—e.g., your supervisor—or to an information source outside your organization.

To determine whether the client is satisfied, check and ensure the information is received and understood. You may need to ask 'does this completely answer your question?'. Encourage clients to return to the reference desk if further help is needed. It is important for clients to know they can return for further assistance if more information is needed, or if they can't locate exactly what they want. You may encourage telephone inquirers or remote users to visit the library if they require further assistance.

Telephone and Virtual Reference

Telephone Reference

It has become common for patrons to access library services without physically entering a library building. Library catalogs are available online and databases allow patrons to search for information on topics and read full-text periodical articles wherever they are, rather than visiting a library to do their research. For some this ability to access services remotely is a convenience; for others, such as the housebound, it may be the only feasible way they can use the library.

When providing reference services from a distance both the requestor and the reference staff member are at a disadvantage. Without face-to-face communication, those clues provided by body language are lost. It is therefore extremely important to listen closely and read between the lines in an effort to pick up verbal and written clues. Just as with the face-to-face interview, patrons may not initially reveal their real information need. Reference interview techniques such as open questions, clarification when necessary, and repetition of the request are vital to verify you have understood the information they require.

Since you are unable to see your patron it is important that you not jump to conclusions about the kind or level of information required. You may need to ask what type of information the user needs and how much depth is required. It may not be possible to determine the age of the person on the telephone by their voice, or in a virtual request by their written language. You could, for instance, make an assumption that you are speaking to a school-age child when in reality they may be a mature person or vice-versa.

Attitude can be reflected in your tone of voice, so be careful to present a positive image. Ross and Dewdney (2013) suggest the following when using the telephone:
- develop a pleasant speaking voice
- identify yourself
- acknowledge what the user said by restating the question
- use minimal encouragers—e.g., "Go on", "Anything else?" so the caller will know you are there and listening
- clarify the question or request by using open questions
- explain what you are doing and give an estimate of how long it will take. Offer to call back if time is a factor
- refer the patron to someone who may be better placed to help if you are unable
- verify key facts before seeking answers
- record messages accurately. Restate names, phone numbers and email addresses as you note them so the caller has a chance to correct any mistakes you may otherwise have made.

Virtual Reference
Libraries also offer email and other written reference options. Here too, some of the concerns and techniques that arise with telephone reference apply. In neither instance can you see your patron's gender, age, or nationality so it is important not to make assumptions. Just as warmth and friendliness should be expressed in your telephone voice, so too should these proprieties come through in your written responses.

Using chat facilities such as *Ask a Librarian* is very similar to instant messaging and not unlike speaking face-to-face. It may not be possible, however, to answer all information requirements during the one chat session, as some questions require further research or referrals to a subject specialist. A live chat session may be used as an introduction to the resources that are available in the library.

It is important to keep the user informed of what you are doing to assist them—even if this means you tell them that you are still looking for information for them.

 Virtual reference requests should not be allowed to pile up. A regular schedule should be established to check for requests and timelines for responding to them.

Tips for Online Reference Interviews

During the online reference interview it is essential for reference staff to keep clients informed of what is happening:
- write in a friendly, conversational but professional manner
- include an explanation of your search process or strategy in your responses
- send information in small portions to reduce the delay in delivery
- let the client know what you are doing regularly so they don't feel abandoned
- if you must be away from your computer, send something for the client to read or consider until you return
- balance between speed and professionalism while adapting to the client's capability
- use correct spelling, grammar, punctuation and capitalization in your responses
- fully cite all resources that are quoted or used in responses
- use the client's name in your responses
- avoid yes/no responses as they could be interpreted as cold and unfriendly
- avoid using jargon but use terminology that is understandable to the client.

Referring Inquiries

In both face-to-face and virtual situations, library staff may sometimes need to refer a reference inquiry to others. Many libraries establish procedures that determine when a reference query should be passed on. These procedures may take into account:
- the length of time needed to solve a query
- how busy the reference staff are
- the intricacies of the query.

An inquiry may need to be referred to a staff member within your own library—e.g., a question might relate to work done in the Technical Services section of the library. It may be necessary to refer an inquiry outside your organization because your library does not have the relevant sources to answer it. For example, you may need to refer the inquirer to the state or national library, or a government department or embassy.

Remember, you do not lose face if you refer a question to other resources. The basic aim of a library is to serve its clients and to fulfil their information needs in the best way possible. Knowledge of other resources and how to exploit them is an aspect of serving clients' information needs.

EXERCISE 3.2

Consider the following requests for information and decide what you would ask the inquirer to start off the reference interview. You do not have to answer the query.

1. Has Felicity Adams written any articles recently about character assassination?

2. Who was Richard Lovelace?

3. What is a Tridon traction splint?

4. Where would I find some up-to-date statistics on Fiji and other countries?

5. Can you find an illustration of the skeleton of a mammal?

In summary, for a successful reference interview:

1. Welcome the client—make eye contact, smile, and give a friendly greeting.
2. Give your full attention and make observant comments.
3. Listen to what the client asks—paraphrase or clarify their question but do not interrupt them.
4. Probe—use open questions to initiate and pursue the inquiry: "Tell me more…." Use contracting questions to narrow the focus "Can you be more specific?"
5. Verify the question by paraphrasing it. Ask "Is this what you'd like to find out?"
6. Search—go with the user to the computer or the shelves, report on your progress (during telephone or virtual requests), and make a referral if necessary.
7. Inform the client—cite the source and confirm that the answer is understood.
8. Follow up—ask "Does this completely answer your question?" or some other appropriate follow-up comment.

CHAPTER THREE   The Reference Interview   27

 **ACTIVITY 3.3**

Role play conducting a reference interview. You will need to work in a group of three to complete this activity.

The person playing the client should ask a general question—e.g., "Does the library have any art books?" but specifically they would like a picture of the Mona Lisa.

The person playing the part of the reference staff member needs to interpret the request for information and offer the client assistance in finding relevant information.

A third person should observe the exchange and take notes of the conversation.

The reference member is to fill in the following self-assessment form and the observer is to fill in the peer assessment form.

Self –Assessment:

Criteria for assessment	Your comments and suggestions on how you might improve your performance
How did you greet the client?	
How did the client respond?	
List two questions you asked.	
How did you determine the client's needs?	
How did you meet the client's needs?	
How did you feel during the reference interview?	
Any other comments or observations you wish to record.	

Peer Assessment:

Criteria for assessment	Competent (note strengths)	Needs more development (indicate areas)
Greeted client appropriately		
Asked appropriate questions to clarify client's information needs		
Adopted communication levels suitable to the client's communication levels		
Provided clear instructions		
Maintained a pleasant and calm manner		
Maintained correct body language and eye contact		
Style of questions asked – open / closed		
Prepared appropriate environment, free of physical barriers		
Checked that client was satisfied with the result		

Legal and Professional Requirements
When assisting a client, you may have to take into account
- copyright
- privacy
- confidentiality
- duty of care
- censorship.

Copyright
Before providing information to a client you must make sure that you are not infringing the copyright laws of your country by copying or downloading information inappropriately. You should become familiar with the conditions of the copyright law and instruct clients on how to comply with it.

Privacy
There can be a fine line between how much a staff member needs to know and the patron's right to privacy in the reference interview. Even if your library is not covered by national or state privacy legislation, libraries generally follow privacy principles such as:
- only collecting the information from a client that is necessary for the library to conduct its business
- not keeping such information longer than is necessary
- keeping that information secure
- ensuring that the client knows what information is being collected, and why.

It is not appropriate to reveal a client's personal details, or the details of an inquiry, to another library client or to other staff who have no need for this information.

In some libraries staff may also need to be aware of commercial, technical, or political reasons for the security and confidentiality of information.

Confidentiality
Library staff must be discreet and tactful when handling inquiries. It can be frustrating when a client is unwilling to tell you why they need particular information, but they have the right to keep their reasons to themselves.

In order to maintain confidentiality, endeavour to conduct reference interviews in a location where your conversation will not be overheard by other library clients.

Duty of Care
Whether or not library staff can be held liable for the quality of the information they supply is not clear. However, when working in a reference area professional ethics require you to make sure that, to the best of your ability, the information you provide is accurate, and comes from a variety of documented sources.

Censorship

Many people argue that libraries should not contain books or other information on controversial topics. However, library associations believe that, within the boundaries set by government legislation, library and information services are responsible for supporting and sustaining the free flow of information and ideas. They consider it important to make available the widest diversity of views and expressions, including those that are unorthodox, unpopular, or considered dangerous by the majority.

EXERCISE 3.4

Examine the following requests for information and decide whether there are any legal implications relating to the request. You do not have to answer the queries.

1. Where would I find a list of poisons?

2. I am interested in buying an atlas. Which one would you recommend?

3. I am appearing in court next month on a drink-driving charge. Can you direct me to some useful legal books?

4. I need to photocopy three chapters out of this book *Techniques for student research*. Can you direct me to the photocopier?

CHAPTER FOUR
The Search Strategy

Introduction
The *search strategy* is the process of finding answers to reference questions in the fastest and most efficient way. This can only be accomplished when the reference interview (discussed in Chapter Three) is done well. Once you have determined what your client actually needs you can begin the search for information. How you go about finding the answer (your search strategy) will direct the process and the specific resources you will use.

One of the challenges of reference work is that no two questions are identical because each client's information need is unique. Many questions require analytical and lateral thinking to locate appropriate information at the right level for each client.

Planning the Search Strategy
Once you have completed the reference interview, think about the kind of information that is needed to answer the question. Then consider how you might look for relevant information. Spending time in the initial planning stages may save you time and effort when looking for suitable resources. It is also likely to assist you in finding more relevant results. Following the steps outlined below should help you to create a successful search strategy.

Search Strategy Overview
Here is a good general approach to creating a search strategy:
- Break down complex questions into more manageable parts. See if the question can be restated or organized differently to find a suitable answer.
- Think broadly about the resources that might satisfy your patron's information need.
- Start with a dictionary or encyclopedia (in either print or electronic form) to provide some background information if needed.
- Review the reference tools that are available in the library to determine what would be most appropriate. Remember to consider books, journals, online databases, government reports, etc. Consider whether there are specific online resources that would relate to the topic.
- Use keywords and subject headings that are appropriate for the reference tools. Use broader terms and synonyms to expand into further information and narrower terms for more precise searching. Remember that differences between British and American terminology and spelling may impact on your searches (particularly when searching online)—e.g., 'colour' or 'color'; 'aeroplane' or 'airplane'.
- Know how to use the available reference tools, including those online.

- Don't rely on just one search engine. Conduct your search using a few search engines and compare the results.
- When examining a reference tool, browse the table of contents and index for appropriate terms. If it contains a user guide, read through it for additional details on how to use the tool.
- Consider the format or media that is most suitable for the user.
- Involve others when necessary. Don't hesitate to search for experts in the field or refer to a local expert. Going to another staff member, making phone calls to potential experts, networking, or asking others may provide a richer and more complete answer for the user.

 Ensure that you understand the patron's real question first, then use a search strategy that will allow you to find the most appropriate resources.

Choosing Information Resources

When you are familiar with your library's collection it is much easier to develop a search strategy. Think about the kind of information that is needed to guide you to the reference tool that will be the most suitable.

Detailed information about reference tools is provided in following chapters. As a general guide, however:
- if you need overview information an encyclopedia would be useful
- for the latest academic research a recent journal article would be more up-to-date than most books
- official international reports are available from international organizations such as the United Nations or the World Bank.

The Search Strategy Process

An effective search strategy involves the following steps:
1. clarify the problem
2. prioritize sources and select materials
3. locate sources
4. search materials
5. evaluate the process
6. compile and present the findings

Clarify the Problem
- fit the topic into a discipline (e.g., ancient history, literature); look up terminology in a dictionary or encyclopedia if needed
- confirm the level of detail needed
- confirm how much information is required
- check if a particular format is needed (e.g., a DVD or a periodical article).

CHAPTER FOUR   The Search Strategy

Prioritize Sources and Select Materials
- decide if the information is likely to appear in reference sources
- identify sources in the order of their likelihood to contain the information
- check if the information is in the library or will require a referral to another organization
- determine if you need to contact an expert in the field.

Locate Sources
- find appropriate resources in the reference or general collections, or online
- identify resources outside the library
- arrange pick up, delivery or access, as appropriate.

Search Materials
- search resources until an answer is found
- if information is not available try to determine why:
    - search different reference tools
    - refer the user to another library or librarian as appropriate.

Evaluate the Process
- analyze the information gathered
- ensure you have fully answered the query, with appropriate detail at an appropriate level for the user.

Compile and Present the Findings
- use the method of presentation required—e.g., verbal answer, list of references, annotated bibliography, etc.
- acknowledge the sources used by citing references in a suitable style.

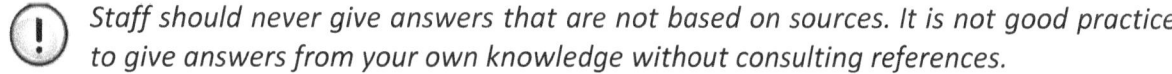

Staff should never give answers that are not based on sources. It is not good practice to give answers from your own knowledge without consulting references.

Exercise 4.1

Choose one of the topics below, and complete the following using the resources in a library. Describe your search strategy.

Refugees	Nelson Mandela
Battle of the Boyne	Climate change
The Great Barrier Reef	Black curlews
Mountaineering	Graphic design
French cookery	Biochemical engineering

1. Find background information on your topic using a library's reference collection. Name the sources you used.

2. Locate two websites or other online resources on your topic. Write down the details and URL for each of these resources.

3. Locate two books on your topic using the library catalog. Write down the bibliographic details and the call number for each book and check whether the items are on the shelf.

4. Find the bibliographic details for two periodical articles on your topic using one of the electronic databases available in your library.

Implementing a Search

When beginning a search, underline the key words or phrases in your client's information request and use these as a starting point for basic search terms and concepts—e.g., 'Discuss the relationship between <u>inflation</u> and <u>unemployment</u>'. Consider if there are other words, phrases or concepts related to, or more appropriate than your initial terms.

Once you have identified key concepts, search for these in the sources you selected in your search strategy. Search processes that are relevant to specific resources will be explained in more detail in the later chapters of this text, which focus on individual types of reference tools. In general, search print resources by using alphabetical index entries, tables of contents, chapter headings, and back-of-book indexes. Online or database searching involves some additional search functions, which are outlined below.

Search Functions

When using different search engines or databases, you may have to format your search strategies in different ways. The following is a general guide to alternative ways of formatting your search strategies. Before you conduct a search in an unfamiliar search engine or database use its 'Search Help' or 'Search Tips' page to find out the correct syntax to use.

Basic Search Features

While individual search engines and databases may have their own unique features, in general the following basic rules apply when searching.

- **Capitalization** doesn't matter (e.g., 'United States of America' and 'united states of america' are considered to be the same search).
- **Order**. Most search engines and databases search for all the words in your search in any order (e.g., if you type in 'new zealand sky tower' the search engine will look for all of the pages with the word <u>new</u>, the word <u>zealand</u>, the word <u>sky</u> and the word <u>tower</u> anywhere in the page but not necessarily in that order).
- **Quotation marks** can be used to make most search engines and databases search for a phrase as a single unit (e.g., typing "new zealand sky tower" with double quotation marks will retrieve pages that discuss the New Zealand Sky Tower as a single unit rather than the separate words in the search).
- **Stop words** are not searched by most search engines or databases. These are insignificant words that appear in a database record or web page. Common stop words include: a, an, the, in, of, on, are, be, if, into, which. However, stop words can vary in different databases. Check the 'Help' screens for the relevant list of stop words in the database or search engine being used.

Advanced Search Features

Using an advanced search option allows you to conduct a more focused search, and narrows the number of hits. Techniques that can make a search more precise are outlined below. Not all of these techniques work in every search engine or database, so check the 'Help' link in the search engine or database for more information.

- **Boolean operators**: are connecting words placed between search terms to narrow or expand a search.
    - **AND**—helps to narrow a search. It tells the computer that both terms must be present in the record (e.g., fruit AND vegetables).
    - **OR**—helps to broaden a search. It is used for like or synonymous terms. Using it tells the computer that either term must be present in the record (e.g., fruit OR vegetables).
    - **NOT**—helps to narrow a search. It eliminates an unwanted search term or group of search terms from the search results (e.g., fruit NOT vegetables).
- **Truncation**: broadens your search to take into account plurals, various word endings and spellings. To use truncation, enter the root of a word and put the truncation symbol at the end. The database will return results that include any ending of that root word (e.g., child* = child, childs, children, childrens, childhood). Truncation symbols may vary by database but common symbols include: *, !, ?, or #.
- **Wildcards**: substitute a symbol for one letter of a word. This allows you to adjust for variations in spelling within a word (e.g., wom?n = woman, women; or defen?e = defense, defence). Not all search systems allow wildcard searching but for those that do, '?' is the most common wildcard symbol.
- **Phrase searching**: Most databases allow you to specify that adjacent words be searched as phrases. Using parentheses or double quotes around search words is a common way to do phrase searching (e.g., "phases of the moon") but not all databases or search engines use them.
- **Proximity operators**: Many databases allow you to specify that the words you are searching are close to each other in the record or document. The proximity operators vary according to the database, but some common ones include:
    - 'w#' = with. It specifies that words appear in the order you type them in. Substitute the # with the number of words that may appear in between the words (e.g., 'tax w3 reform' tells the computer 'tax' and 'reform' must appear in this order in a document, but can be up to 3 words apart).
    - 'n#' = near. It specifies that the words may appear in any order. Substitute the # with a number of words that may appear in between the words. (e.g., 'tax n3 reform' tells the computer 'tax' and 'reform' can appear in any order in a document, and be up to 3 words apart).
- **Nesting**: with a complicated search, you can put the various parts in parentheses, to make it easier for the computer to understand. This is useful when you are mixing ANDs and ORs (e.g., (fruit OR vegetables) AND (cereals OR grains)).
- **Fields**: contain specific pieces of bibliographic information in library databases. Common fields include: author, title, journal title, abstract, publisher, date of publication and subject. Limiting your search to specific fields can yield more precise results. To find various fields within a database, look for drop down boxes or menus to select the field you want to search. Then combine words and fields together with Boolean or proximity operators for a more precise search.
- **Limiting**: is another way to make your results more specific. Many of the same Field options (discussed above) are able to be used as limits, however, limit options will vary between databases. For example, you may only want to retrieve full-text articles or limit your results to articles published in certain years.

- **Searching for information from a specific site**: if you need information from a specific site, you can limit the search to a type of site (e.g., .edu or .gov) or to a specific domain (e.g., edu.ph). You do this by using the term 'site:' in the search (e.g., history AND site:edu.ph). This works in Google and some, but not all, other search engines.

Relevance Sorting

The results of a completed search need to be looked at to select the information that will be most relevant. Search engines and databases rank the results using some of the following criteria to determine relevance:

- **proximity**: how close the search terms are
- **frequency**: a page that has the term(s) mentioned a lot will rank higher than pages that mention it only once or twice
- **completeness**: for search engines that do not require every term to appear, pages with all of the terms will rank higher than pages with only some of them
- **locations**: most search engines can tell where the terms appear and increase the rank of a page with the terms in the title or section headings above pages where the terms just appear in the body
- **links**: some search engines examine the links to the page to increase the rank of pages that have more links from similar pages
- **date**: databases will often present resources in chronological order—often by the date published but sometimes according to when they were added to the database.

While you may not be able to determine which of these relevance criteria your search engine or database is using, it is important to realize that something is happening in the background. You might like to try similar searches using more than one search engine to see if one ranks resources that are useful to you in a different order from another search engine.

Use the 'Help' screens to find out how to combine search terms, what truncation and wildcard symbols to use, and what other search features are available on that database.

Tips for Online Searching

1. **Plan your search strategy**
   Make sure you understand what kind of information you require. Select the concepts and then identify keywords or subject terms that will describe them.

2. **Select your database**
   Select the most relevant database/s for your search.

3. **Perform your database search**
   Search the database using your concepts, keywords or subject terms.

4. **Evaluate the results**
   Look at your search results. Look at the citation abstracts and subject headings. Are they relevant? Identify those citations that will be useful.

5. **Do you have too many results?**
   - Check your use of OR and AND.
   - Use the database filtering options. For instance do you need a particular publication type, or specific date range?

6. **Do you have too few results?**
   - Try adding other search terms and combinations.
   - Have you found recurring subject headings that you could use?
   - Are there more synonyms for your keywords?
   - Use truncation or wildcard features.
   - You may need to edit your search several times to retrieve the most relevant citations.
   - If you have expanded the search as far as you can and are still not getting enough results, try searching on another database in the subject area.

7. **Save the search results**
   Use print, email, save or export options.

8. **Locate the full-text**
   - If you are searching a full-text database, click on the link to get to the article.
   - If the database doesn't contain full-text articles, take a note of the citation and search to see if you are able to access the article elsewhere. It may be necessary to check print journals or ask for an article on interlibrary loan.

9. **Refine your results**
   After you have completed your search, if you did not find relevant results or need to find more, you should:
   - check your spelling
   - consider using alternative keywords/subjects e.g., use 'sweets' or 'lollies' as well as 'candy'
   - use alternative spellings such as 'organization' OR 'organisation'
   - use truncation symbols or wildcards to capture all forms of your keywords
   - check that you have used Boolean operators correctly
   - search other databases.

   If you found too many references, you could narrow your search or make it more specific:
   - add another concept and associated keywords
   - restrict your search to specific fields such as 'abstract'
   - add search limiters to your search such as 'date range' or 'peer reviewed'.

10. **Evaluate your search**
    After conducting your searches, display the search results and evaluate them to see if they match your topic.

EXERCISE 4.2

Go to http://www.google.com and select 'Advanced search' from the 'Settings' menu on the bottom task bar. Complete the following searches. Use the template provided with each question to plan your search.

1. I would like brief information about a breed of cattle known as Belted Galloways.

Find **pages** with	**all** these words	
	this **exact** word or phrase	
	any of these words	
	none of these words	
Site or Domain	Only return results from the site or domain, e.g., *google.com, .org*	

2. I am looking for a description of the symptoms of someone who has contracted the ebola virus.

Find **pages** with	**all** these words	
	this **exact** word or phrase	
	any of these words	
	none of these words	
Site or Domain	Only return results from the site or domain, e.g., *google.com, .org*	

3. I need reliable information on Edwards Syndrome. I need a brief explanation of what it is.

Find **pages** with	**all** these words	
	this **exact** word or phrase	
	any of these words	
	none of these words	
Site or Domain	Only return results from the site or domain, e.g., *google.com, .org*	

4. Are there Canadian support groups for parents of children with attention deficit disorder?

Find **pages** with	**all** these words	
	this **exact** word or phrase	
	any of these words	
	none of these words	
Site or Domain	Only return results from the site or domain, e.g., *google.com, .org*	

Techniques for Good Searches

Whether using print or online tools, reference staff should:
- consider the most suitable sources of information that are available on the topic (including the library catalog, reference collection, general collection, online resources, databases, people, other libraries and organizations)
- watch out for spelling mistakes or any factual errors
- search all possible spellings
- watch spacing, as hyphenated words may be written in different ways, e.g., yearbook or year book
- search related terms such as synonyms
- look for existing bibliographies on the topic when conducting a literature search, as these could save time and effort
- consult the *Library of Congress subject headings* (LCSH) or other appropriate subject headings to determine related terms and synonyms as well as broader and narrower terms
- keep a record of the search strategy, showing the lines of inquiry followed and any trails not followed or not completed.

REVISION QUIZ 4.3

Use the following questions to revise your understanding of the search strategy. You do not need to write down the answers.

1. What is a search strategy?

2. List four aspects to consider in your general approach to creating a search strategy.

3. Name five components of the search strategy process.

4. What basic search features could you use when conducting searches?

5. Name five advanced search features that may assist you in conducting a more focused search.

Notes:

CHAPTER FIVE
Introduction to Reference Tools

Introduction
A reference collection contains resources in print and electronic format intended to be referred to rather than read. These resources are often known as *reference tools* or *reference works*. This chapter will present a general overview of reference collections and reference tools. Later chapters in this text will deal with specific types of reference tools in more detail.

The reference collection consists of encyclopedias, dictionaries, biographical resources, directories, yearbooks, almanacs, atlases, gazetteers, manuals, handbooks, bibliographies and other sources providing readily accessible reference information. Reference tools need to be available at all times, so they are usually not for loan. Reference collections are arranged to enable convenient use by library clients and staff.

Characteristics of Reference Tools
Resources used for reference purposes are a special category of material with distinctive characteristics:
- reference tools are meant for consulting to find specific information, and not for consecutive reading
- information is organized in reference tools to provide fast access to the material in the most convenient manner possible
- reference tools are mainly secondary or tertiary sources that summarize, interpret and/or analyze primary (i.e., original contemporary) documents
- reference tools are usually compiled from a large number of sources. They gather together existing information rather than creating new knowledge.

Finding Out about Reference Tools
In order to find out what reference tools exist and what they cover, you can look at:
- published guides to reference sources (printed and online)—e.g., *New Walford's guide to reference resources*
- sections or chapters of books on reference work that deal with reference tools—e.g., Cassell and Hiremath, *Reference and information services in the 21st century: an introduction*
- resources listed or reviewed on websites—e.g., *Book reviews in the reference trade* (Oxford University Press Canada, http://www.oupcanada.com/); Books Monthly website (http://www.booksmonthly.co.uk/nonfic.html)
- reviews of new reference works in journals and newspapers—e.g., the *Library Journal*'s 'LJ Reference Reviews' in each issue; reviews in *Australian Academic and Research Libraries* (AARL), *New York Times Sunday Book Reviews* or *Canadian Book Review Annual online*

44   LEARN REFERENCE WORK

- special issues of library journals—e.g., an annotated list of outstanding reference works is published annually in the May issue of *American Libraries*
- announcements from publishers about forthcoming reference tools
- online booksellers—e.g., http://www.encyclopediacenter.com specializes in all types of reference books; http://www.amazon.com and other generalist booksellers have 'reference' categories
- guides to reference tools in subject areas—e.g., *Reference sources in the social sciences and humanities* at UCLA Library
- 'library research guides' for works in a specific library's reference collection—e.g., *Research guides at the State Library of Victoria*
- information on websites of special reference divisions of professional library associations—e.g., RUSA website (*The Reference and User Services Association*, a division of the American Library Association); The *Library and Information Research Group* site of CILIP.

Activity 5.1
The list above shows the types of resources you can use to find out about reference tools. Choose some of these and identify at least two tools that are new to you. List details of the tools below. What sources did you use to find these reference tools?

Evaluating Reference Tools
When choosing reference material, either to buy or to use, consider the following factors:

- currency
- accuracy
- authority
- aim or purpose
- scope
- bias or slant
- arrangement
- bibliography
- quality of index
- format
- need
- cost

Currency

It is important to check the preface or introduction of a reference tool to determine the timeliness of the information. The year of publication is not always an indicator of the currency of the contents as some reference sources take years to compile. The copyright date is a better indication of major revisions. Resetting the text of a reference source, such as a large encyclopedia, is a major undertaking so some publishers produce yearbooks or a supplement instead of updating the complete work.

Web resources are easily updated but one cannot assume that everything on the Web is current. Check websites for details of when pages were last updated. Updating schedules are important factors when considering all types of resources.

Accuracy

Accurate information is essential when providing a reference service to users. Spot check facts in resources and consult reliable reviews to confirm the quality of information. Accuracy may be sacrificed if the author or editor relies solely on secondary sources.

Some reference tools are designed to be eye-catching, using lots of colors, large illustrations, maps, and a variety of fonts. It is important not to be sidetracked by presentation and forget to check the accuracy of the information.

Authority

The publisher's reputation is important and can be used as a measure of the quality of the work. The preface of a print resource, or the 'about' section of a web tool, usually lists names of editors, editorial staff, advisers, consultants and contributors and includes their qualifications and status.

Aim or Purpose

Most reference tools include an introduction that explains why the work was produced and describes the intended client group. Read the Introduction to ensure the work will be useful for your collection.

Scope

Check to see whether the publication is comprehensive within its chosen area or whether it is selective. Some reference sources are designed for specialists. Others are designed for the popular market. Authors or editors may compromise between scholarship and popularity to boost sales.

Bias or Slant

Some reference tools have a national, political, or group slant. They may include information of interest to a particular country, party, or organization rather than having a generic appeal. Always check where a reference work was published, as this may suggest a bias in the presentation.

Arrangement
Some reference tools are easier to use than others because the information is arranged in a more logical manner. Most clients want to find information quickly so they prefer sources designed for ease of consultation. Arrangement and presentation are important.

Bibliography
Reference sources often provide bibliographies or suggestions for further reading. It is important to check the recency of these references.

Quality of Index
Printed reference tools should always contain an index. The index should be comprehensive and easy to use. It should include adequate cross-references pointing to related entries, and 'see' references from non-used terms. Electronic resources should include index-type features like hyperlinks or good keyword search facilities.

Format
Features of print resources such as the size of the publication, typeface, illustrations and maps, paper quality and colors, the style of binding and the total arrangement will all influence your judgement of a reference work. The inclusion of special features such as maps, charts, illustrations, tables, photographs and bibliographies may encourage staff to use one reference source in preference to another.

The format of electronic resources should also be considered: packaging (online, DVD, USB, etc.), typeface, resolution clarity of illustrations, and special features can be determining factors in choosing an electronic resource.

Need
It is important to consider how the item relates to your reference collection. Is the material needed to provide balance or to complement other available resources? Does it fit the needs of the users? The same information is often available in print or electronic form. The subject matter and the intended use will help determine the best choice for the situation.

Cost
Cost can be a factor when choosing reference tools; however, pricing alone should not be the determining factor in purchasing. All libraries have budgets and there is never enough money. You should always consider the purchase of a new reference tool in relation to the needs for the collection as well as the restrictions of the budget.

Evaluating Electronic Reference Sources
There are numerous advantages to using electronic reference tools:
- ease of updating information
- ease of cross-referencing by the use of hypertext, allowing the user to click on a word for further or related information
- links to external sources—websites, articles etc.—to provide quick access to additional material

- addition of animation, video, and audio to enrich the information experience
- keyword and Boolean searching
- inclusion of editorial updates and revisions—this is most useful for evaluating currency of information
- access to information available 24/7.

There can also be disadvantages—e.g., unsolicited pop-up advertising.

Many of the factors to think about when evaluating printed reference tools also apply to electronic reference sources. Additional criteria to consider are:
- **special features**—Electronic resources have the capacity to provide a richer experience using audio and video features, links to other material, etc. Is the resource taking advantage of these technologies, or simply providing a pdf file of a text-based resource?
- **quality of reproduction**—How clear are maps, diagrams, illustrations? Are 'zoom' features available without loss of resolution? Are audio features easy to hear and understand? Do video clips download quickly? Do links to other material work, and are they maintained over time?
- **ease of searching and navigation**—How sophisticated are the search facilities provided—are there keyword and advanced search options? Is there a contents page with navigation links? Is an index included as well as search capabilities? Do all navigation links work?
- **advertising and affiliations**—Is the site free of advertising? If the reference work is on a site sponsored by a particular organization, is the reference tool objective and impartial—or does it reflect the views and possible bias of its parent body?

Examining Reference Tools
- Study the title page or online equivalent carefully to determine the scope of the work as indicated in the title, the author's name, the author's background (qualifications, positions held, titles of earlier works), the publisher and the date of publication.
- Read the preface or introduction for further information about the scope of the work, special features, limitations if any, and comparison with other publications on the subject.
- Check through the resource to determine its arrangement, types of entries, cross references, supplementary lists, indexes and the quality of articles. Notice if articles are popular or scientific, signed or unsigned, impartial or biased. Check to see if bibliographical references are included. For online resources, the 'Help' screens can provide some of this information.
- Compare the reference tool with earlier editions. Is it a major revision or simply a minor upgrade? Does it supersede earlier editions, or act as a supplement to be used in conjunction with the older resource?

EXERCISE 5.2

Visit a library and select any general reference tool. Examine it carefully, using the steps above. Make notes in the form below and add comments for features you want to remember.

Title	
Author or editor (if there is one)	
Author's qualifications/background	
Edition	
Place of publication, or Website URL	
Publisher and Date of publication	
Purpose and scope of work	
Special features (if any)	
Arrangement (e.g., alphabetical list)	
References, lists, indexes or Quality of articles (if any)	
Additional comments	

Ready Reference Tools

Some reference tools are used for what is termed *ready reference* work. They are designed to answer basic factual questions like:
- What is another word for aggregate?
- Who is the Prime Minister of England?
- Where is Angora?
- When was the Boer War?

Ready reference tools are often used for the following:
- quick (and usually) short answers
- factual rather than analytical information
- facts located in a single source
- overview rather than in-depth information.

Ready reference tools can be print publications, but they are increasingly becoming available online. Many library sites provide links to online ready reference tools—an Internet search for 'online ready reference' will bring you to both generalist ready reference tools, and those useful for specialist subject areas.

Types of ready reference tools include:
- **almanac**—an annual calendar with astronomical and other data; a miscellany of useful facts and statistical data
- **atlas**—a volume of maps or charts with or without explanations
- **bibliography**—a list of related resources, usually subject-related
- **biographical dictionary or biographical directory**—an alphabetical listing of people containing their life dates, titles, birthplace, family, education, and career highlights
- **dictionary**—an alphabetically arranged publication containing information about words, meanings, derivations, spellings, pronunciation, syllabication and usage
- **directory**—a list of names of residents, organizations or firms in a city, region, country or international group, providing various details such as address, telephone number, email, and website; also, a list of members of a particular profession or trade
- **encyclopedia**—a systematic summary of significant knowledge; or a summary of knowledge of one subject. Usually arranged alphabetically
- **gazetteer**—a geographical directory listing information on places and locations
- **handbook**—a concise ready reference source of information for a particular field of knowledge
- **manual**—a book of instruction on doing, making, or performing something
- **yearbook**—an annual publication containing current information in brief, descriptive and/or statistical form.

50   LEARN REFERENCE WORK

 EXERCISE 5.3

Find an example of each of these tools in your library's reference collection. Note how the work is arranged and the information it contains. Fill in the tables below.

Dictionary—an alphabetically arranged publication containing information about words. (Use an English language dictionary for this exercise.)

Title of dictionary	
Author or editor (if there is one)	
Edition	
Place of publication, publisher, date of publication	
Call number or URL	
Purpose of work	
Arrangement (e.g., alphabetical listing)	
Example of a question it might answer	

Encyclopedia—a systematic summary of significant knowledge.

Title of encyclopedia	
Author or editor (if there is one)	
Edition	
Place of publication, publisher, date of publication	
Call number or URL	
Purpose of work	
Arrangement (e.g., alphabetical listing)	
Example of a question it might answer	

Biographical dictionary/directory—a listing of people providing details such as titles, birthplace etc.

Title of biographical dictionary	
Author or editor (if there is one)	
Edition	
Place of publication, publisher, date of publication	
Call number or URL	
Purpose of work	
Arrangement (e.g., alphabetical listing)	
Example of a question it might answer	

Directory—(1) a list of names of residents or organizations in an area, providing addresses, email, phone numbers etc.; (2) a list of members of a particular profession or trade.

Title of directory	
Author or editor (if there is one)	
Edition	
Place of publication, publisher, date of publication	
Call number or URL	
Purpose of work	
Arrangement (e.g., alphabetical listing)	
Example of a question it might answer	

Atlas—a volume of maps or charts with or without explanations.

Title of atlas	
Author or editor (if there is one)	
Edition	
Place of publication, publisher, date of publication	
Call number or URL	
Purpose of work	
Arrangement (e.g., alphabetical listing)	
Example of a question it might answer	

Gazetteer—a geographical directory listing places, locations and information about them.

Title of gazetteer	
Author or editor (if there is one)	
Edition	
Place of publication, publisher, date of publication	
Call number or URL	
Purpose of work	
Arrangement (e.g., alphabetical listing)	
Example of a question it might answer	

CHAPTER FIVE   Introduction to Reference Tools   53

Yearbook—an annual publication of current descriptive and/or statistical information.

Title of yearbook	
Author or editor (if there is one)	
Edition	
Place of publication, publisher, date of publication	
Call number or URL	
Purpose of work	
Arrangement (e.g., alphabetical listing)	
Example of a question it might answer	

Almanac—a miscellany of useful facts and statistical data.

Title of almanac	
Author or editor (if there is one)	
Edition	
Place of publication, publisher, date of publication	
Call number or URL	
Purpose of work	
Arrangement (e.g., alphabetical listing)	
Example of a question it might answer	

Manual—a book of instruction on doing, making or performing something.

Title of manual	
Author or editor (if there is one)	
Edition	
Place of publication, publisher, date of publication	
Call number or URL	
Purpose of work	
Arrangement (e.g., alphabetical listing)	
Example of a question it might answer	

Handbook—a concise source of information for a particular field of knowledge.

Title of handbook	
Author or editor (if there is one)	
Edition	
Place of publication, publisher, date of publication	
Call number or URL	
Purpose of work	
Arrangement (e.g., alphabetical listing)	
Example of a question it might answer	

CHAPTER FIVE   Introduction to Reference Tools   55

Bibliography—a list of related resources, usually subject-related.

Title of bibliography	
Author or editor (if there is one)	
Edition	
Place of publication, publisher, date of publication	
Call number or URL	
Purpose of work	
Arrangement (e.g., alphabetical listing)	
Example of a question it might answer	

Selecting the Correct Reference Tool

To select the correct reference tool for ready reference work, remember the basic questions: *what? who? where? when? why?* The table below will help you choose the best tools to consult.

Information Sources

Question		Purpose	Source
What?	Words	Meaning Spelling Pronunciation Synonyms Usage	Dictionaries, thesauri
	Things	Background	Encyclopedias
		Facts and figures	Almanacs, handbooks
Who?	People	Background	Biographical dictionaries Encyclopadias
		Location	Directories
Where?	Places	Location	Maps, atlases, gazetteers
		Facts and figures	Almanacs, handbooks
		Background	Encyclopedias, thematic atlases
When?	Events & dates	Facts and figures	Almanacs, yearbooks
		Background	Encyclopedias
Why?	Information	Current events	Indexes, yearbooks
		Facts and figures	Directories, handbooks, statistics
		Background	Encyclopedias

Adapted from Lane, Nancy, Margaret Chisholm & Carolyn Mateer. (2000). *Techniques for student research: a comprehensive guide to using the library*. New York: Neal-Schuman. Figure 2-2.

EXERCISE 5.4

*Look at the following questions and decide which **type** of reference source to use to find the answer. You do not need to name a specific title, or to answer the question.*

Describe the clues you would look for when deciding how to find the answer—e.g., if the question asks for the meaning of a word you would use a dictionary.

*Of course, the answers to all of these questions can easily be found on the Internet or in print sources, and you will be searching in these sources in later chapters. The aim of this exercise is for you to think about the **type** of source that best fits the information need.*

1. Where is Palermo?

2. When will Easter fall in the year 2020?

3. When was the Battle of Waterloo?

4. What do the initials GATT stand for?

5. When was the actress Elizabeth Taylor born?

6. Who are the members of the Brunei royal family?

7. I need some details about the side effects of psychotropic drugs.

8. I am writing a paper for publication and am not sure when to use quotation marks. Where would I find some instruction?

9. I need some information on environmental pollution for a Grade 6 school project.

10. I am looking for some recent articles on folk medicine.

11. How many children attend private schools in Fiji?

12. Who wrote the series *Game of Thrones*?

13. What are the names of the major companies registered in Rio de Janeiro?

14. Who is the Premier of the Canadian province of Alberta?

15. I want to make repairs on my Toyota Corolla.

 Summarizing the process of choosing appropriate reference tools:

- You must ensure that you understand the query.
- You should be clear about the type of answer that is needed.
- You must be aware of the sources of information that are available.

CHAPTER SIX
Online Resources

Introduction
Whether accessing electronic or print resources, the reference tools used are often the same, but the approach taken in searching them is quite different. For print tools, you must first decide what type of tool will best find the information you require. In online environments, you can search across all sorts of tools to find information. Once the search has been performed, you need to sift the results to find the best type of information resource. The URLs and summary details provided by search engine results will help with this—sometimes the results can indicate the type of tool itself; sometimes the results will show it is a database; sometimes an indication of the type of organization is given in the domain name (this is useful for authoritativeness).

While the chapters following this one discuss a range of reference tools that are available in print and electronic form, this chapter considers periodical indexes, or databases, that are predominantly available in electronic format.

However, as many people use the Internet as their first step in finding information, it is important to begin this chapter with an understanding of how to use the Internet effectively and efficiently to find relevant information.

The Internet
The Internet consists of a huge number of pages that may combine text, graphics, sound, animation and video. These pages are linked to other pages using hypertext (usually indicated by underlining and/or a distinct color). Clicking on hypertext will activate the link, and will transfer you to the linked page.

URLs
All pages on the Internet have a URL (Uniform Resource Locator). This is the address at which the resource can be found. Each URL consists of the following components:

network protocol :// host name / resource location
- network protocol—defines the network that is used to access a resource, followed by the three characters '://'—e.g., **http://**www.loc.gov/library/digitalreference.html
- host name or address—identifies the location where the Internet page is held—e.g., http://**www.loc.gov**/library/digitalreference.html
- file or resource location—contains a path to one specific network resource on the host—e.g., http://www.loc.gov**/library/digitalreference.html**

A typical URL is: http://www.iwm.org.uk/research. This may be decoded as follows:

http://	(hypertext transfer protocol)—tells the computer to transmit data in a format that can be displayed on the Internet. Most browsers do not need you to enter this part of the URL
www	indicates that the site is located on a World Wide Web server, a computer that makes websites and documents available to the network
iwm	indicates the organization whose server it is (in this example it is the Imperial War Museums)
org	indicates the type of website (i.e., an organization)
uk	indicates the country of origin (i.e., the United Kingdom)
research	indicates the path to the research portion of the website

Domain Names

In the example above, 'iwm.org.uk' is an example of a *domain name*. A domain name is that part of a URL that identifies the particular website where this page is located.

Top Level Domain Names (TLDs)
There are a number of top level domain names, the most common being:
- .com   Usually indicates a commercial organization (in some countries .co is used)
- .edu   Educational organizations (in some countries .ac is used)
- .gov   Government bodies (in some countries .govt is used)
- .org   Organizations (nonprofit)

Top level domain names also include two letter country codes:
- .ac   for Ascension Island
- .ad   for Andorra, and so on.

You will note, however, that U.S. websites rarely include the '.us' country code.

For a complete list of Top Level Domains and country codes see *Norid: Domain name registries around the world*, at http://www.norid.no/en/domenenavnbaser/domreg/

It is important that you are able to decode a domain name, to assess the relevance and quality of the website. When looking at this information consider the following:
- Could this site have a country bias?
- Is this site trying to sell me something?
- Does this site come from an academic institution or government department?

EXERCISE 6.1

Without searching for them on the Internet, try to identify the name of each organization represented by the following URLs. What else can you determine about the organization?

1. http://www.gramophone.co.uk

2. http://www.un.org

3. http://www.nytimes.com

4. http://www.sl.nsw.gov.au

5. http://www.up.edu.ph

Evaluating Information on the Internet

Not all pages found on the Internet are of high quality as there are no required standards or rules to be met when publishing a web page. To decide whether the information you find on the Internet is reliable, use similar criteria to that used to assess information found elsewhere. The previous chapter provided factors to consider when evaluating reference tools in both print and electronic form. These factors are equally valid when evaluating information on the Internet.

Authority
- Can the author of the page be determined?
- Is contact information provided (name, email, phone number or address)?
- Is the author affiliated with an organization? Or is the author speaking for himself or herself?
- Are qualifications or credentials for the individual or organization provided?

Objectivity
- Objectivity is related to authority.
- Does the author have a bias or agenda? Is this bias stated or hidden?
- Does the author indicate his or her goal in providing the information?
- Is there a disclaimer included in the pages?

Accuracy/Coverage
- Remember that almost anyone can publish on the Web.
- Is the source of information provided?
- Who is the intended audience?
- What is the focus of the information?
- What is the depth of coverage of the information?

Currency
- Are dates (First Posted, Last Updated) included?
- Is the information current or out-of-date?

Other Considerations
- Does the presentation appear professional (no typos, misspelling)?
- Is the page easy to use and well organized?
- Do the links from the page connect properly?
- Is special software necessary to view the page?

Finding Reference Information on the Internet

There are two broad approaches to finding reference information on the Internet:
- if you know the URL for a particular reference tool, you can navigate directly to that tool, or if you know a website that provides collections of reference tools, you can search that site for an appropriate tool
- you may choose to search for the information directly, by using a web search tool, such as a web directory or a web search engine.

CHAPTER SIX   Online Resources   63

EXERCISE 6.2

Using the webpages of different libraries, answer the following questions about online reference resources.

1. Find out if your library has a webpage with a collection of electronic reference tools. If not, choose another library that has such a page. Take some time to study it and observe which reference tools have been chosen.

2. Browse a university library's reference guide and select tools to answer the following questions. Note the tool that you used:
    a. Who was the goddess Artemis?

    b. What does the acronym FEMA stand for?

    c. On what day of the week will September 11 fall in 2021?

    d. What is the latitude and longitude of Manhattan, N.Y.?

    e. I would like a brief summary of the Nicaraguan economy.

3. Use another collection of electronic reference tools to find *Biography.com*, then answer the following questions:
    a. Why was Eleanor Roosevelt famous?

    b. Where was Genghis Khan born?

    c. Emma Thompson won a BAFTA award for which BBC TV series?

4. Use the *Bartleby.com: Great Books Online* website to find *Bartlett's quotations*, then answer the following questions:
    a. Who wrote *Nearer, my God, to Thee*?

    b. Who said "England expects every man to do his duty"?

    c. Who said "A blessed companion is a book—a book that fitly chosen is a life-long friend"?

Search Engines

Sometimes you may not be able to find a relevant reference tool on the Internet. Therefore, you will need to use a search engine to help answer your question directly. Search engines attempt to index the Internet without human intervention. They rely on a web robot or spider, a program that periodically moves around the Internet, indexing the key words on each page.

Because keyword search engines mechanically index words, not concepts or ideas, a search on a word could return a list with millions of documents containing your keyword. To stem this flood of resources, it is important to plan how you are going to search, using a search strategy and search functions (discussed in Chapter Four) prior to commencing your search.

Types of Search Engines

There are many types of search engines. One such type is a search engine that is embedded in a website, e.g., the Library of Congress's website at http://www.loc.gov/ has a facility to search that site. This tool is useful when you know the site you want.

Some engines search within a specific subject e.g., *Justia* (http://www.justia.com/) for law or *iMedisearch* (http://www.imedisearch.com/) for medicine. In general, these subject directories are smaller and more selective than other search engines.

The most popular type of search engine is a universal search engine that tries to index the entire contents of the Internet, for example *Google* (http://www.google.com) or *Bing* (http://www.bing.com). Because keyword search engines mechanically index words, not concepts or ideas, a search in one of these search engines can return a huge number of 'hits' or results. When using one of these, it is best to develop a search strategy that will limit your search.

Other search engines allow searching for a specific type of media. For example, to search for information on maps, *Google Maps* (http://www.google.com/maps/) would be a good starting point. When searching for videos, a search on *YouTube* (http://www.youtube.com/) would be a logical beginning.

Limitations of Keyword Search Engines

There are many keyword search engines that contain different features, and (unfortunately) different techniques for each one that the user has to learn. You should not rely on one search engine alone if you are serious about your research. Because of differences in software, different search engines may retrieve different sets of documents from the same search, with varying degrees of overlap.

When conducting reference searches, it is appropriate to search across a number of keyword search engines. This will ensure a more thorough coverage of the topic. Be aware, however, that you will need to conduct your search differently in each search engine, so it is a good idea to read and learn the instructions for each search engine that you use.

EXERCISE 6.3

Find information on the following topics using several different search engines, such as http://www.bing.com or http://www.ask.com or http://duckduckgo.com.

1. I am looking for brief information about encephalitis.

2. I am looking for a description of NASA's future missions to Mars.

3. I need accurate information on the Nuremberg trials.

4. I would like to know what Sriracha is and what it is used for?

Electronic Resources

An *electronic resource* is any resource that is available in an electronic format. Information resources are increasingly being made available as electronic resources on the Internet. Electronic resources can include websites, online databases, e-journals, e-books and electronic integrating resources, available as audio, visual, or text files. Although many electronic resources are free, a significant number of electronic reference tools are user-pays services.

Subscriptions to electronic resources are often expensive, so libraries must choose the titles most appropriate for their users. Providing access to these resources requires an understanding of the technology as well as licensing and pricing agreements. License agreements define who is authorized to use the resources and how many users can have access at the same time. These agreements also specify whether users can have remote access to resources and what a user is able to do with the content. Consortia arrangements involving multiple library systems, multi-type libraries, statewide licensing, and multi-state agreements are constantly developing and changing.

In general, most agreements provide library patrons with access to e-resources for their educational and research needs. Commercial use is generally not allowed under the terms of licensing agreements. Below is a list of what is, and is not, allowed when it comes to using electronic resources.

Allowed	Not Allowed
For education and research	Share material with unauthorized users
Save, download, and/or print portions or single copies	Post material via the Internet or listservs
Share with colleagues in same organization	Share user IDs and passwords with unauthorized users
Avoid commercial or for profit use	Use to support the activities of a business or an organization, both profit and non-profit
Link to specific resources	Engage in automatic downloading of large amounts of content
Give proper acknowledgement to your sources	Remove copyright or intellectual property notices

Bibliographic Databases

A *bibliographic database* is an electronic collection of references to published resources that is searchable. It generally requires an online subscription to access information from sources such as journal and newspaper articles, conference proceedings, reports, government and legal publications, and other reference works. The contents of these resources are regularly and systematically indexed and included in the database. Some databases may also include videos, audio files, podcasts, blogs, and images. Since the information found in these types of resources is published more quickly than information found in monographs, this is a good place to commence your search for current material. Bibliographic databases may enable users to locate terms too recent or concepts too narrow to be identified in printed sources. Entries found in a bibliographic database contain a bibliographic citation, including details such as: the author, if available; title of the resource; publication details i.e., publisher, date of publication; and a description of the content of the resource in the form of an abstract or subject headings. Resources are accessed using subject or keyword searches.

 Read documentation associated with the database, e.g., 'Help' screens, before starting a search.

Bibliographic databases may be either:
- general—covering many periodicals in a wide subject field such as:
    Academic search premier
    Readers guide to periodical literature
- subject-specific—covering many periodicals in a particular subject area such as:
    Education source
    CINAHL complete

Not all library databases are bibliographic. Some of the more common databases you may be familiar with include:
- **library catalogs**—index all of the resources owned or subscribed to by a particular library. In general, catalogs describe books and journals as a whole, not individual chapters or articles
- **article indexes**—index individual articles within specific academic fields. The journals and books indexed by these databases may or may not be online or available at one specific library
- **online collections**—e-journals and e-books that are either grouped by the publisher or collected into subject specific packages by content aggregators.

Some online services allow the user to search one database at a time. In others, a group of databases can be searched together.

Abstracts

Abstracts provide a summary of the contents of each resource included in a database. The lengths of abstracts vary, depending on the database, from a few phrases to a detailed paragraph.

In general, databases contain three basic types of abstracts:
- *indicative abstract*—a short abstract written to enable readers to decide whether or not they should read the original article or publication
- *informative abstract*—a summary of the principal arguments and information of the original publication or article. It can serve as a substitute for the original publication
- *evaluative abstract*—comments on the worth of the original article or publication.

Full-Text Databases
Many databases provide the full text of the journal articles they index, as well as the citation details. The availability of full-text articles will depend on the subscription agreements each library has with publishers and content aggregators.

Access to full-text articles can save hours of time searching for the article in print or electronic form, or trying to obtain the journal article through interlibrary loan.

Hyperlinks
Within some databases you will see hyperlinks included. If an author's name is hyperlinked, clicking the link will provide citations to other articles by the same author. Hyperlinked subject headings can be especially helpful in finding similar articles on your topic.

Selecting the Right Database
In order to use the right database it is important to know what it contains. Some of the important points to consider include:
- subject area—note what subject areas are covered to ensure that you are using the correct database for your topic
- date range—there is often a specific cut-off date for content in a database, as they will often cover resources published in the last few decades. If you are looking for articles or research from before that date, you will need to use a different database. Databases of historical resources may not include current journals. Some databases exclude the most recent year or two of all journal articles.
- types of material—most databases index scholarly journal articles, but some will include specific types of content (such as: magazine or newspaper articles; books; book chapters; dissertations; conference papers; statistical data; images, audio, or video)

Steps in Using a Database
1. **Choose and define the topic**—make a list of the subjects or keywords that describe your topic
2. **Choose an appropriate database**—ask reference staff, get recommendations from others or look at relevant reference resources for suggestions
3. **Find instructions on how to use the database**—for online indexes, use the 'Help' information
4. **Plan a search strategy**—this can ensure an efficient search
5. **Search the index**—look up key words or subjects in the index. Compile citations for the articles you think may be suitable
6. **Check whether full-text articles are available**—If they are, select and read those most appropriate to your topic
7. **Search for journals not available in full-text**—check the library catalog to see if the relevant journals are available from your library and note how to access them.

A major advantage of searching databases is being able to combine search terms and to access multiple fields in the same search.

When searching any database be aware of the concepts related to efficient use—precision and recall.

- Precision indicates the effectiveness of the search—specifically the ratio of relevant documents retrieved to the total number of documents retrieved.
- Recall indicates the ratio of the total number of relevant documents in the database to the number of relevant documents retrieved.

EXERCISE 6.4

Find answers to the following questions using appropriate databases that you are able to access.

1. Find a full-text review of one of Robert Ludlum's books. List the title of the book, the database used, and the citation for the full-text article.

2. Find an article on childhood diabetes. Give the full citation.

3. Identify a database appropriate to use for research in psychology.

4. Find an article about CPI inflation. Give the full citation of the article and the title of the database used.

5. Name two databases covering education. How are they different?

6. Identify a database that contains public health information. How can you access it?

7. Where can you find the ERIC database? What does ERIC stand for?

8. Name a general periodical database. Find a library that provides access to the database.

9. Find an article about John Steinbeck. Include the name of the database and the full citation of the article.

10. A user wants information on the Alaska earthquake in the 1960s. Find an article and provide the name of the database and full citation of one article.

CHAPTER SEVEN
Dictionaries and Encyclopedias

Introduction to Dictionaries
A dictionary is an alphabetically arranged publication containing information about words, meanings, derivations, spelling, pronunciation, syllabication and usage. It may also give synonyms, antonyms, illustrative quotations, maps and plates, biographical facts and geographical information. The word 'dictionary' comes from the Latin *dictio,* meaning a word or a phrase.

Most people are familiar with general usage dictionaries. There are also dictionaries dealing with virtually every language and subject, and special purpose dictionaries—e.g., dictionaries of slang, rhyming words, acronyms and abbreviations, new words, obsolete words, names, phrases, quotations, or dictionaries to aid special groups like crossword enthusiasts.

Library classification systems place dictionaries with language. Dictionaries of English language are classified in Dewey Decimal Classification (DDC) in 420. Library of Congress Classification (LCC) puts English language dictionaries in PE. Specialized dictionaries are generally classified by subject. Most dictionaries will be found in reference collections although older editions may be moved to the general collection.

Uses of Dictionaries
Dictionaries are used in reference work to check the meaning, pronunciation, and spelling of words. They may be used as a guide to correct grammar, to find out usage of words, or to explain the origin of a word. Dictionaries are useful in preparing a literature search or answering a reference question on an unfamiliar subject.

Categories of Dictionaries
Language dictionaries are frequently categorized according to the number of words listed:
- unabridged: over 250,000 words
- semi-abridged: 130,000 - 250,000 words
- abridged or concise: 55,000 - 130,000 words
- pocket: under 55,000 words
- children's/school: 25,000 - 95,000 words.

They can also be grouped by type:
- historical: give the history of the use of a word
- etymological: focus on the origin of a word and how it changes over time
- foreign language: dictionaries in other languages
- bilingual: provide equivalent words in two languages
- subject: cover a given topic or discipline.

Other Word Tools
Other reference tools beside dictionaries can deal with word issues:
- **book of quotations**—a list of well-known quotations arranged chronologically, alphabetically by author or keyword, or by subject. Printed works will typically have several indexes to provide maximum access. Electronic formats are readily available. Examples include *Bartlett's familiar quotations*
- **book of usage**—a work that describes correct use of terms and words, particularly words that are easily confused such as 'accept' and 'except.' One of the most popular books of usage is *Fowler's modern English usage*, often simply referred to as Fowler's
- **concordance**—an alphabetical index of all the important words in a book, or in the works of an author, with references to the phrases and passages in the text. Examples include concordances to the Bible, or for a particular author such as Shakespeare or Chaucer
- **glossary**—an alphabetical list of definitions. The list may relate to words used in a particular book or to a particular subject. Generally glossaries are found at the end of a book such as this textbook. In some cases glossaries are published separately, for example *LibrarySpeak: a glossary of terms in librarianship and information management*
- **lexicon**—a wordbook or dictionary, most often of ancient languages—e.g., Greek, Hebrew and Arabic. The term is derived from the Greek *lexis* meaning word and is frequently used in the title, for example *A Greek-English lexicon of the New Testament and other early Christian literature*
- **style manual or style guide**—guidelines or standards for setting out references and bibliographic citations, as well as for the writing (grammar, punctuation, etc.) and design of documents. An example is the *Chicago manual of style*
- **thesaurus**—a work containing synonymous and related words and phrases rather than explaining meanings. The word thesaurus (plural *thesauri*) is of Greek origin and means a storehouse or treasury of knowledge. The term thesaurus is used to describe dictionaries that arrange words and their synonyms in classified order and not in the usual alphabetical order. One of the most well-known is *Roget's thesaurus*. Special subject thesauri are slightly different—they are controlled vocabularies used in database indexing, that focus on relationships between the concepts expressed by the words.

Terms Associated with Words or Wordbooks
Reference collections may also contain specialist dictionaries or word books dealing with:
- **antonyms**—opposites; e.g., 'good/ bad', 'soft/hard'
- **conundrums**—riddles whose answer is or involves a pun
- **crosswords**—there are dictionaries specifically prepared for crossword puzzle users
- **dialects**—books showing regional use of language by variation of grammar or pronunciation
- **eponyms**—words based on a person's name, e.g., 'braille', 'peach melba'
- **name books**—books indicating the meanings of both first and last names
- **new words**—some dictionaries publish supplements of new words periodically
- **orthography**—the conventions of correct spelling, hyphenation and capitalization
- **obsolete words**—books or lists of obsolete words

- **palindromes**—words or groups of words that read the same backward or forward; e.g., 'pep'; 'toot'; or 'name no one man'
- **puns**—the humorous use of a word to suggest two meanings or the meaning of another word similar in sound
- **synonyms**—different words for the same or similar thing; e.g., 'dust jacket' and 'book cover'.

EXERCISE 7.1

Look for an example of each of the following types of dictionaries and list their titles below. Find as many as you can in your library; seek out the rest via a physical or online bookshop.

1. General (abridged or unabridged)

2. Children's

3. Synonyms and antonyms

4. Slang

5. Usage

6. Abbreviations and acronyms

7. Subject (these include highly specialized words)

8. Foreign languages

9. Crossword

10. Obsolete words

11. New words

12. Names

13. Quotations

14. Rhyming

15. Eponyms

Examining a Dictionary
Dictionaries usually have the following components:
- **preface**—stating the aim and the scope of the publication
- **key to abbreviations**—a list of abbreviations used in the body
- **key to pronunciation**—using the phonetic alphabet or re-spelling words using the ordinary alphabet
- **body**—the main sequence of words, usually in alphabetical order. Alphabetizing may be word-by-word or letter-by-letter. The content of entries gives information such as origin, history and usage
- **appendices**—supplementary sequences of words to update the main sequence or deal with special categories of words such as meanings of first names. Some dictionaries include encyclopedic information such as weights and measures, lists of royalty, chemical compounds, etc.

Most people who consult a dictionary never read its instructions on use. You should examine all sections of a dictionary in order to use it fully and efficiently.

Dictionaries are likely to include the following details about a word:
- spelling—with preferred variants
- syllabication—division into units of pronunciation
- pronunciation—the way the word is spoken
- part of speech—verb, noun, adverb, etc.
- etymology—origin of the word
- definition—the exact meaning
- synonyms—a word or phrase meaning exactly or nearly the same
- antonyms—a word or phrase opposite in meaning
- illustrative quotations—to show how a word is used
- usage labels— slang or obsolete notation
- abbreviations—as appropriate
- illustrations—pictures or diagrams.

Some dictionaries may include other features such as:
- biographical names
- foreign words and phrases
- forms of address
- geographical names
- signs and symbols.

EXERCISE 7.2

Choose three of the following words and compare their definitions in three different dictionaries. Use at least one different type of dictionary in each case.

fierce	patch
stalwart	doll
retire	combine
nick	case
inhale	fantastic

Evaluating a Dictionary

Consider the following to determine if the dictionary will suit your users' needs:
- **authority**—this is determined by the reputation of the compiler and the publisher
- **ease of use**—a good dictionary should be well-presented and simple to navigate, with keys to its usage and information on its purpose, scope and features. Print dictionaries should use clear typefaces that can be read easily
- **word coverage**—word coverage may be limited because it is impossible for a general dictionary to be comprehensive without becoming excessively large. Therefore, a dictionary needs regular updating to include new words and changes in usage
- **word treatment**—it is important to know how a dictionary treats its words. Does it give etymology, quotations and illustrations? Are the definitions clear, accurate and up-to date?

Selecting a Dictionary

When deciding which dictionary to use for answering a reference question:
- **listen to or read the question carefully**. Look for keywords that will help you determine the source to use. For example, in the question "Who said 'Frankly my dear, I don't give a damn'?" the keywords *'who said'* indicate your source should be a dictionary of quotations.
- **clarify the information required**. For example, does the inquirer want a meaning of a word or its origin?
- **check for associations with languages or countries**. Is the word used in specific countries? Does this give clues to the origin of the word—e.g., that it derives from a particular language? Do you need to check national, bilingual or polyglot dictionaries?

EXERCISE 7.3

Choose examples of dictionaries in print or electronic form from the list below or from works you find on your own. Fill in the details for five titles. Select a variety of types.

- *Acronyms, initialisms and abbreviations dictionary*
- *Bartlett's familiar quotations*
- *Black's legal dictionary*
- *Brewer's dictionary of phrase and fable*
- *Fowler's dictionary of modern English usage*
- A dictionary for children, from any country
- *Chambers dictionary of science and technology*
- *Oxford English dictionary*
- *Shorter Oxford English dictionary*
- *Roget's thesaurus / Roget's international thesaurus*
- *Webster's third new international dictionary (USA)*, or
- *Macquarie Dictionary (Australia)*
- A dictionary of slang, from any country

1. Title

    Place, publisher, date

    Intended user group

    Arrangement

    Special features

2. Title

    Place, publisher, date

    Intended user group

    Arrangement

    Special features

3. Title

    Place, publisher, date

    Intended user group

    Arrangement

    Special features

4. Title

   Place, publisher, date

   Intended user group

   Arrangement

   Special features

5. Title

   Place, publisher, date

   Intended user group

   Arrangement

   Special features

EXERCISE 7.4

*Suggest a **type** of dictionary (e.g., a medical dictionary) likely to provide the answers to the following questions. You do not have to answer the questions, or give an exact title or bibliographic details for the dictionary.*

1. What is herpetology?

2. What is the origin of the phrase 'son of a gun'?

3. What does the acronym GUBU stand for?

4. What is the meaning of the medical term axilla?

5. What is the difference between elemental and elementary? How should these words be used?

6. I am looking for a word with a meaning similar to peaceful.

7. When was the word 'lurch' first used?

8. 'Skite' is a word used in Australian slang. What does it mean?

9. What is the Spanish word for handkerchief?

10. Who said 'a man will turn over half a library to make one book'?

EXERCISE 7.5

Find the answer to these questions using a dictionary. Name the source.

1. Can you find a synonym for the word intellect?

2. When was the word break-neck first used?

3. Find examples of how the word son-in-law was used in the 1800s.

4. When would I use the term imaginary instead of imaginative?

5. What is the scientific instrument called an integrating meter?

6. What is a pea jacket?

7. What is a Lincoln rocker, that was named after the U.S. President, Abraham Lincoln?

8. What is the French word for laugh?

9. What is the meaning of the medical term coryza?

10. Who was described in the quote 'mad, bad and dangerous to know'?

Introduction to Encyclopedias

An encyclopedia is a systematic summary of all significant knowledge, or a summary of the knowledge on one subject. All encyclopedias are selective to some extent. They may be in a single volume or a multi-volume set. A single volume cannot give depth of coverage, but it is useful for factual information and less expensive than a multi-volume set.

Along with dictionaries, encyclopedias are the most frequently consulted ready reference tools. Their primary use is to search for specific facts—to answer *'who?, what?, when?, where?* and *how?'*. They are often the first step toward a more extended search.

General encyclopedias are usually classified together in the reference collection. Libraries using the Dewey Decimal Classification (DDC) shelve general encyclopedias in 030 while those using Library of Congress Classification (LCC) place them in AE. Subject encyclopedias are classified according to subject, and are therefore dispersed through the reference collection.

Characteristics

Encyclopedias provide background information, and are not usually intended for the subject specialist. Articles are written by subject experts and adapted by editorial staff. Articles signed by the contributors are more likely to be authoritative. Most articles include a bibliography listing further reading.

Encyclopedias can be international and broad-ranging in coverage, or focus on a specific subject or discipline. Many countries produce national encyclopedias, highlighting information about the country's history, culture, events, people, places, politics, science and sport. These are written in the language or languages of the country. Some general international encyclopedias are available in multiple foreign language translations. Some encyclopedias—e.g., *Encyclopaedia Brittanica*—are scholarly in language and approach while others like *World Book Encyclopedia* are designed for use by school children and their parents and therefore adopt a more 'layman's' style.

It is important to keep encyclopedias current. Most encyclopedias adopt a policy of continuous revision. Approximately 10-15% of the content is updated annually, and topics involving current events are updated more frequently. Some publishers issue yearbooks to update the main sequence, or supplements for particular regions.

Uses

An encyclopedia may be used to provide the following information:
- brief factual details where there is little controversy
- an introduction to or an overview of a topic for the novice
- referral to more detailed works through a bibliography at the end of the article.

 When using an encyclopedia always read the introduction to find out its strengths and features as well as how the information is organized.

An encyclopedia is often the first source used by those seeking factual information. When the required information is not contained in the encyclopedia, the list of readings may lead to other sources.

EXERCISE 7.6

Browse a reference collection to find a print example of each of the following types of encyclopedias. List their titles below.

a. General encyclopedia

b. National encyclopedia

c. Foreign language encyclopedia

Find five examples of subject-specific encyclopedias and list their titles below.

1.

2.

3.

4.

5.

Electronic Encyclopedias

Many encyclopedias are available electronically—on disk or via the Internet. Electronic formats can enhance content by adding animation and sound effects. Use of hypertext also permits easy cross-referencing: a reader clicks on an indicated word to find further information.

In selecting and evaluating an electronic encyclopedia consider the following:
- Is the encyclopedia based on a printed version, even if it has a different name?
- Is the information up-to-date?
- Are the pictures and sounds relevant to the particular article?
- Is the name of the contributor given?
- Is there a bibliography or further reading?
- Is the information easy to find?

Wikipedia

The electronic encyclopedia most often consulted is *Wikipedia* (http://www.wikipedia.org), which differs from other reference tools in significant ways. It describes itself as a 'free-content' encyclopedia based on a model of openly editable content. The encyclopedia is a collaborative effort based largely on volunteer contributors. Anyone can contribute material to *Wikipedia*, and it has grown swiftly to over six million entries in many languages since it was created in 2001, adding new articles every day.

A new entry is often written by an enthusiast rather than an expert, so new articles can be inaccurate or contain serious errors or bias. However, because so many people use and contribute to *Wikipedia*, errors can be identified and repaired promptly.

Not everyone is convinced of the value of Wikipedia, as evidenced by the article *Should I use or cite Wikipedia?—Probably not* (http://library.williams.edu/citing/wikipedia.php) on the Williams College Libraries, USA, website. Since there is no central control over the selection of topics, *Wikipedia* can overlook important issues or treat them too briefly. Again because style is not imposed, the quality of the writing varies. The creators of *Wikipedia* are aware of these defects, and try to take steps to address them. Like the articles in it, *Wikipedia* itself is a continual work in progress.

EXERCISE 7.7

Choose two of these topics:

Architecture	Pompeii
Mexico City	Sikhs
The Red Cross	Jane Austen
Trombones	Halley's Comet
Albert Einstein	Weightlifting

Compare entries for your topics in the following encyclopedias, or in encyclopedias you find on your own:

- *Encyclopaedia Brittanica* (print and/or online versions)
- *World Book Encyclopedia* (print and/or online versions)
- *Wikipedia*

Consider these points in your comparisons:
- How large is the article?
- Are there links to other topics?
- When was the article written?
- Who wrote it?
- What sort of reader is it written for?

Topic 1:
Encyclopedia 1

Encyclopedia 2

Wikipedia

Topic 2:
Encyclopedia 1

Encyclopedia 2

Wikipedia

Selecting an Encyclopedia
When deciding which encyclopedia to use for answering a reference question:
- **listen to or read the question carefully**. Decide if the information is likely to be in a general or a subject-specific encyclopedia.
- **determine how much information is required**. Some questions can be answered adequately using a general single-volume encyclopedia (e.g., "Where was Alexander the Great born?") However, if a list of campaigns in which Alexander fought and a description of the major battles including maps of the battlefields is required, a more detailed encyclopedia such as *Encyclopaedia Britannica* may be needed.
- **decide if the question indicates a particular subject or country**. For example, if information is sought on a technical topic, a scientific rather than a general encyclopedia might be more appropriate; if the question is country-specific a national encyclopedia can be consulted.
- **think about how recent the required information must be**. A current affairs question is more likely to be addressed online than in print.

EXERCISE 7.8

Choose examples of encyclopedias in print or electronic form from the list below or from works you find on your own. Fill in the details for five titles. Does your library hold these titles, or similar ones in the subject area?

- The Canadian encyclopedia
- The Columbia encyclopedia (print version), or Columbia electronic encyclopedia http://www.infoplease.com/encyclopedia
- Encyclopedia Americana
- Encyclopaedia Brittanica
- The Encyclopedia of Australian architecture; or any art, architecture or design encyclopedia
- Encyclopedia of library and information sciences
- Encyclopedia of religion and nature, edited by Bron Taylor; or any encyclopedia of religion
- Encyclopedia of the Central Intelligence Agency by Thomas Smith Jr, or The Central Intelligence Agency: an encyclopedia of covert ops, intelligence gathering and spies by Jan Goldman
- International encyclopedia of the social and behavioral sciences
- World Book encyclopedia

1. Title

    Place, publisher, date

    Intended user group

    Arrangement or search options

    Special features

2. Title

    Place, publisher, date

    Intended user group

    Arrangement or search options

    Special features

3. Title

    Place, publisher, date

    Intended user group

    Arrangement or search options

    Special features

4. Title

   Place, publisher, date

   Intended user group

   Arrangement or search options

   Special features

5. Title

   Place, publisher, date

   Intended user group

   Arrangement or search options

   Special features

EXERCISE 7.9

*Suggest a **type** of encyclopedia (e.g., an Australian encyclopedia) likely to provide the answers to the following questions. You do not have to answer the questions, or give an exact title or bibliographic details for the encyclopedia.*

1. Where is Amritsar? What is it famous for?

2. My child is very interested in elephants and would like some background reading on this topic.

3. When was the Royal Flying Doctor Service of Australia established?

4. Who wrote the American national anthem *The Star-Spangled Banner*?

5. I am writing an essay on nuclear structure and need some information on this topic.

6. I would like a complete list of the works written by Charles Dickens and detailed information about his influence on English literature.

7. I would like to know the history of the Québec Winter Carnival.

8. A graduate student is writing a thesis on the family in society and would like to find detailed information on this topic, including a bibliography of relevant publications.

9. What does a gorilla eat?

10. I would like some information about the Mafia in Sicily for my Italian-speaking uncle.

EXERCISE 7.10

Find the answers to these questions using an encyclopedia. Name the source.

1. I want some information on Alaskan folklore.

2. Sir Alexander Fleming won the Nobel Prize for Medicine in 1945. Who shared the prize with him?

3. I am a psychologist and need current views about cognitive development and its effects on behavior.

4. I am about to start my thesis on East Asian decorative arts and would like some background information.

5. My primary school child needs some information on the Olympic Games.

6. Where can I find an encyclopedia article on libraries and archives in Asia?

7. Does the library have any information on the theory of social control?

8. Where would I find detailed information on rocket propulsion?

9. I am a specialist nurse and would like background information on bone marrow disorders.

10. Where would I find a comprehensive article and reading list of books on linguistics?

CHAPTER EIGHT
Organizational, Biographical and Trade Directories

Introduction
Some information queries are best answered using specific types of reference tools. Details about people and organizations are found in *directories*.

Directories are usually kept in the reference collection but may be placed under subject rather than format. The Dewey Decimal Classification provides number-building directions to indicate directories of persons and organizations. General directories in Dewey collections may be in the 000s; Library of Congress libraries classify general directories in AY.

In order to be effective, a directory should:
- be current and updated regularly
- allow easy retrieval of information
- include sufficient information for comprehensive coverage
- provide uniform entries.

Arrangement
Directories are easy-to-use reference tools. Generally arrangement is in one of several ways: alphabetical by name or subject, geographical, or numerical by some code. Entries are usually concise and easy to understand although some print directories abbreviate entries extensively and it may be necessary to consult the key to abbreviations.

With printed directories, variations in alphabetical order may be confusing. Entries can be word-by-word or letter-by-letter. The difference is that spaces come before letters in word-by-word arrangement; spaces are disregarded in letter-by-letter arrangement. Many directories use word-by-word arrangement but if an entry is not found, letter-by-letter order should be checked.

 It is important to examine an unfamiliar directory closely before use, because the content and arrangement can vary.

Finding a Directory
In addition to the sources noted in Chapter Five's section 'Finding out about Reference Tools', directories can be found by using a directory of directories. These are available in print form and online—e.g., *WDR directory of directories* lists a range of directories on the Internet; *Engineering.com* focuses on organizational directories in the engineering field.

Organizational Directories

Organizational directories are the major source of information about organizations. They may cover businesses, commercial and non-profit companies, government agencies, educational institutions or other types of organizations.

Most directories list organizations alphabetically by the name of the organization, with a subject index. Some are arranged by subject with an alphabetical index under name. Organizational directories include details such as the full name of the organization, address, contact information (telephone, email, fax, website), names of personnel or office bearers, the function or purpose, and additional information such as a brief history, date of establishment, activities, services and publications.

Information is usually collected by sending questionnaires to organizations eligible to appear in the directory. The accuracy of the data depends on the responses of those surveyed. A form may be sent requesting updates on a regular basis or when there are changes to an organization's details.

Because organizations change frequently, many directories are now produced in electronic format and made available on the Internet. Electronic directories have the advantage of providing multiple access points and frequent updates.

There are hundreds of directories and there may be several covering the same subject field.

Uses

Directories are used to identify and contact organizations. Companies use directories to identify potential clients, trading partners or investment opportunities. Not-for-profit agencies use directories to compile mailing lists of potential supporters. Students use directories to find information about educational institutions and their courses. Researchers use directories to find current information about organizations and associations. Older directories may be useful for historical research.

Selecting an Organizational Directory

When a library selects a directory to acquire, the following factors should be considered in addition to accuracy, currency and coverage:
- **relevance**—does the directory cover organizations important to the library users?
- **political and economic factors**—are the organizations listed affected by changing national and international circumstances? Will this influence how often the directory is updated?
- **quality**—is the information provided extensive and comprehensive? Is the layout simple to follow and are the entries easy to understand? Do electronic resources have links to further information, for example about organization officials or associated companies?
- **authority**—who produced the directory? Are the producers well-regarded in the subject field?
- **cost**—if a print product, how often is a new edition published? How will this impact on the reference budget? If an electronic resource, what is the subscription price?

EXERCISE 8.1

Choose examples of organizational directories in print or electronic form from the list below or from works you find on your own. Fill in the details for five titles.

- *American library directory* (print or online)
- *Australian government directory* http://www.directory.gov.au/
- *Directory of Latin American universities and colleges* (via the website titled '4 International Colleges & Universities') http://www.4icu.org/Latin-America/
- *Directory of New Zealand libraries* https://natlib.govt.nz/directory-of-new-zealand-libraries;* or any directory for a country or type of library, print or online
- *Directory of public companies in United States* http://www.crmz.com/Directory/CountryUS.htm
- *Dun & Bradstreet 'Who owns whom'* (any region of the world)
- *European business directory* http://www.europages.com/
- *Guide to giving* (Australian directory to non-profit organizations, print or online) http://www.probonoaustralia.com.au/directory#
- *Innovation, Science and Economic Development Canada (formerly Industry Canada)* http://www.ic.gc.ca/eic/site/icgc.nsf/eng/h_07063.html
- *International literary market place*
- *Lincs—Local Information Network for Community Services* http://www.datadiction.com.au/lincs/
- *Nationwide business directory Australia* http://www.nationwide.com.au/
- *Official museum directory*
- *UK Community Planning Consultants* portal http://www.communityplanning.net/consultants/consultants.php
- *United Kingdom government* https://www.gov.uk/
- *World of learning* (Europa)
- *WRTH – World radio TV handbook*

1. Title

   Publisher, copyright date, last updated

   Intended user group

   Arrangement or search options

   Special features

2. Title

   Publisher, copyright date, last updated

   Intended user group

   Arrangement or search options

   Special features

3. Title

   Publisher, copyright date, last updated

   Intended user group

   Arrangement or search options

   Special features

4. Title

   Publisher, copyright date, last updated

   Intended user group

   Arrangement or search options

   Special features

5. Title

   Publisher, copyright date, last updated

   Intended user group

   Arrangement or search options

   Special features

EXERCISE 8.2

*Suggest a **type** of organizational directory (e.g., a business directory) likely to provide the answers to the following questions. You do not have to answer the questions, or give an exact title or bibliographic details for the directory.*

1. Which colleges offer education courses by distance education?

2. What is the circulation of the *Toronto Star* newspaper?

3. How many people are members of the Australian Trombone Association?

4. When was Oxford University founded?

5. I need a list of book publishers in Eastern Europe.

6. I need basic information about the Golestan Palace Museum in Iran: address, collections, etc.

7. I am looking for a directory of dentists. Does one exist?

8. How many people work for the company Searchscene?

9. What is the purpose of the Canadian Consumers Association?

10. Which company owns New Zealand's Cloudy Bay Wines?

EXERCISE 8.3

Find the answer to these questions using an organizational directory. Name the source.

1. I would like a list of magazines about disability issues published in the United States.

2. Who is the President of the Addis Ababa University in Ethiopia?

3. What is the name of the parent company of Hino Motors Vietnam Ltd.? What is the address (street, city, country) of the parent company?

4. Does the University of Technology in Jamaica offer bachelor degrees in engineering?

5. Is the *Scientific Bulletin of Naval Academy* available as an open access journal?

6. What are the contact details for the Byblos Bank Europe in Belgium?

7. What literacy programs and services are available in Florida?

8. How many libraries are there in Rotorua, New Zealand?

9. Who is the contact person for Save the Children Australia?

10. What products are available from the Canadian company Forest Gold Products Ltd.?

Biographical Directories

Biographical directories contain information about the lives of people. They may include details of a person's full name, gender, date and place of birth, a summary of their achievements, details about their personal life (e.g., family, interests), memberships, employment history including publications, offices and positions held, honors, awards and contact details. Some include pronunciations of names, portraits or photographs, and bibliographies leading to more detailed information.

General biographical reference tools are classified in the 920s for libraries using Dewey Decimal Classification (DDC) and in the CTs for those using the Library of Congress Classification (LCC). Subject-specific biographical tools are often classified with the subject.

Characteristics

Biographical directories are often called *biographical dictionaries*. Their coverage may be all-inclusive, or confined to:
- country
- gender
- occupation or profession
- living or deceased people.

Print versions of biographical dictionaries are usually arranged alphabetically by surname. Online versions provide more options for finding information. Most include basic searching facilities—e.g., 'search' by name keyword or alphabetical 'browse' by surname. There may also be advanced search options for locating people by country, occupation, etc. Most online biographical dictionaries are Internet-based. Some may be accessed at no charge, others are databases available through subscription.

Online biographical dictionaries can also link users to additional sources—e.g., the subject's website, articles from newspapers or journals, social media sites, etc. As with other online reference tools, these directories can be quickly and easily updated, thus increasing the likelihood of information remaining current.

When creating biographical dictionaries, publishers may rely on historians or subject experts to collect and verify biographical information, using primary sources. They may send questionnaires to the people they want to include in their directory. Information may be updated by directly contacting individuals or via templates on the publisher's website.

Authority of Publishers

It is important to check the authority of a publisher. Most people have heard of 'Who's who' and believe these are produced by a reputable source. In reality, the title 'Who's who' is in the public domain and can be used by any author or publisher. The definitive, authoritative range of 'Who's who' and 'Who was who' resources are published by A&C Black, an imprint of Bloomsbury Publishing in Britain. The online versions are published by Oxford University Press. A series of *Who's who* focusing on America are published by Marquis and are widely used in the United States, although they have been dogged by controversy about whether they are 'vanity' publications, where purchase of the work is a condition of being included. Other 'Who's who' titles and their publishers should be carefully checked to avoid purchasing vanity publications. Similarly, some online directories are 'wiki'-style publications, where anyone can create entries for themselves or about others. These should be cross-checked if possible to determine the accuracy of entries.

Uses

Biographical dictionaries are used for concise summaries of facts about people. They usually focus on life dates, areas of expertise, and key achievements. While most of the information contained in biographical dictionaries can now be found in various online sources, the structured presentation in a biographical dictionary makes it easier to find details that could be 'buried' in the texts of online information sources. For example, a Google search for 'Judi Dench hobbies' will return many sites, and somewhere in their text might be information about some of Dench's hobbies. However, the biographical dictionary *'Who's who'* has a 'recreation' category that succinctly lists all the hobbies, submitted by Dench herself.

Types of Biographical Directories

Universal or International

These include entries for people from all countries, and may be limited to notable public figures rather than including sports personalities or film stars. They may include living and/or deceased people and sometimes biblical, mythological or legendary people. Examples include *International who's who* (available in print and online subscription), *Chamber's biographical dictionary* (print only), *Biography.com* (online only).

National or Regional

These include entries for people from particular countries, states or local areas. They may cover people from all walks of life, living or dead. Examples of regional directories focusing on living people include Oxford University Press' *Who's who* (British people), *Canadian who's who* (only living Canadians), and Marquis' *Who's who in America*. Examples of retrospective directories (i.e., including deceased subjects) are the *'Who was who'* series for various parts of the world.

Many directories calling themselves 'national biographies' focus only on deceased people of national significance. Examples include *American national biography, Dictionary of Canadian biography, Australian dictionary of biography, Biographical database of Australia, Oxford dictionary of national biography.*

Subject, Occupation or Special Characteristic

These concentrate on a particular subject (e.g., science), occupation (e.g., medicine) or special characteristic (e.g., gender). Examples include *Notable American women: a biographical dictionary, International who's who in music, Biographical directory of the United States Congress, Complete dictionary of scientific biography, Sporting heroes (http://www.sporting-heroes.net/).*

Social Media Networks

There are numerous social media sites that provide biographical information in a directory format. Professional networking sites like *LinkedIn, Viadeo* or *XING* cover all occupations. Some sites focus on specific topics or characteristics, e.g., *Doximity* (for medical personnel), *Women's Network Australia, ineedabookkeeper.com* or *iseekLAW.com*. Many professional association websites include directory information, sometimes open to the public, e.g., *Indexers Available* from the various indexers' societies—and sometimes only for the use of their members, e.g., *Epernicus* (for research scientists). Biographical information can also be found on general social media sites like *Facebook*.

Selecting a Biographical Dictionary
When deciding which biographical directory to use:
- **listen to or read the question carefully**. Is the person alive? Most *Who's who* publications include the living, whereas dictionaries of national biography or a title such as *Who was who* include only deceased subjects. The titles of biographical reference materials often indicate the coverage. *Who's who* and *Who was who* are British; *Who's who in America* and *Who was who in America* are American, etc.
- **determine the nationality or the profession of the person** to narrow the search and assist in choosing an appropriate tool
- **identify the type of information needed** such as brief facts, an essay, current or retrospective periodical articles about the person, or a whole book.

Other Sources of Biographical Information
Biographical information can also be found in other sources. If detailed information is required you can consult resources such as:
- encyclopedia entries for prominent people
- dictionaries with special biographical lists
- the library catalog, that will lead you to material written by or about the person
- indexes to journal articles, or *Biography index* for biographical material in articles
- periodicals devoted to biographies, e.g., *Current biography magazine*, with 14-18 biographical essays on people of 'contemporary importance' per issue, 11 issues per year
- online reference databases, e.g., *Biography in context*, a Gale publication providing biographies for historical and current figures world-wide taken from journal and newspaper articles, videos, audio and images
- newspaper obituaries
- almanacs.

 Remember to check any source of information for authority, accuracy and currency.

EXERCISE 8.4

Choose examples of biographical directories in print or electronic form from the list below or from works you find on your own. Fill in the details for five titles. Try to choose some titles from each group.

Web-based directories
- *Australian dictionary of biography* http://adb.anu.edu.au/
- *Australian biography online* http://www.australianbiography.gov.au/
- *Biographical database of Australia (BDA)* http://www.bda-online.org.au
- *Dictionary of New Zealand biographies* http://www.teara.govt.nz/en/biographies
- *Dictionary of Canadian biography* http://www.biographi.ca/en/index.php
- *S9.com biographical dictionary* http://www.s9.com/
- *Bio or Bio.com* http://www.biography.com/
- *Sporting heroes* http://www.sporting-heroes.net/

Directory databases by subscription *(if your library has access)*
- *Who's who*—any title, e.g., *Who's who in Australia* http://connectweb.com.au/pages/whos-who-in-australia.aspx
- *Current biography* http://www.ebscohost.com/academic/current-biography-illustrated
- *Biography in context* http://solutions.cengage.com/InContext/Biography/
- *Oxford reference online* http://www.oxfordreference.com/
- *Oxford dictionary of national biography* http://www.oxforddnb.com/
- *American national biography* http://www.anb.org
- *Canadian who's who online* https://www.canadianwhoswho.ca/order-subscribeonline.php

Print directories *(or others found in your library)*
- *Chambers biographical dictionary*
- *Current biography magazine*
- *Who's who*—any title, e.g.,
  - *International who's who* published by Europa/Routledge; or
  - *Who's who in Australia* published by ConnectWeb

1. Title

    Publisher, copyright date, last updated

    Intended user group

    Arrangement or search options

    Special features

2. Title

    Publisher, copyright date, last updated

    Intended user group

    Arrangement or search options

    Special features

3. Title

    Publisher, copyright date, last updated

    Intended user group

    Arrangement or search options

    Special features

4. Title

    Publisher, copyright date, last updated

    Intended user group

    Arrangement or search options

    Special features

5. Title

   Publisher, copyright date, last updated

   Intended user group

   Arrangement or search options

   Special features

CHAPTER EIGHT   Organizational, Biographical and Trade Directories   105

 EXERCISE 8.5

*Suggest a **type** of biographical directory (e.g., a British biographical dictionary of the living) likely to provide the answers to the following questions. You do not have to answer the questions, or give an exact title or bibliographic details for the directory.*

1. I need a list of films directed by Francis Ford Coppola, the American filmmaker.

2. When did Samuel L. Katz, American professor of pediatrics, serve as instructor in pediatrics at Harvard Medical School?

3. Who was Guy Fawkes?

4. Where was Pope Francis born?

5. Where would I find out how to pronounce the name Hamerik, a 19th to early 20th century Danish composer?

6. When did Queen Elizabeth II succeed her father King George VI to the throne?

7. What is Walter Rudolf Hess known for?

8. When did Rudyard Kipling die?

9. Where is Horatio Nelson, the English naval commander, buried?

10. Where can I find background information on the actor Denzel Washington?

EXERCISE 8.6

Find the answer to these questions using a biographical directory. Name the source.

1. When did Christopher Columbus first reach the New World?

2. Sir Wilfrid Laurier was the first French Canadian prime minister. What years did he serve in the Assembly of Quebec?

3. When was Maria Sharapova appointed as a UNDP Goodwill Ambassador?

4. What are the middle names of Rt. Hon. David Cameron, the former Prime Minister of the United Kingdom?

5. What is the title of the first film made by François Truffaut, the French film director, who died in 1984?

6. In what universities has Canadian poet and novelist Margaret Atwood worked?

7. What are the names of actor Robert Downey Jr's children?

8. What is the nationality and profession of Khaled Hosseini?

9. What was the posthumous publication of Sir Terence Pratchett?

10. What years was William Richard Hawkey the Director and Professor of Music at the Australian National University?

Trade Directories

Trade directories, also known as trade bibliographies, are produced by commercial publishers, and are primarily intended for book retailers. The purpose of trade directories is to provide information about recently published resources.

Each trade bibliography most commonly focuses on one form of material—books, periodicals, spoken word DVDs, computer software, and so on. There is often a national or regional emphasis in each publication, although some directories aim to be international. As with other bibliographic tools, trade directories are available in print and some are available online by subscription.

Characteristics

The place and date of publication (and sometimes the language) are the main factors that determine the scope of trade directories. Other factors may be the form of publication, such as books or periodicals, and the kind of issuing agency, such as trade publishers.

Trade directories do not have a uniform arrangement. While online trade directories are searched using nominated access points, printed trade directories are arranged in a wide variety of ways. This includes:
- dictionary arrangement, with authors, titles and subjects in one alphabetical listing (e.g., *Cumulative book index*)
- alphabetical by name of publisher (e.g., *Publishers' trade list annual*)
- alphabetical in two indexes: (1) by author and editor, and (2) by title and series (e.g., *Books in print*)
- alphabetical by subject (e.g., *Subject guide to Books in print*)
- classified (e.g., by Dewey Decimal Classification, as *American book publishing record*)

The content of trade directories also varies but may include:
- price of the resource at the time of publication
- descriptive annotations
- lists of publishers and their addresses
- titles in trade series (i.e., those from a single publisher)
- evidence that a book was in print when the trade directory was issued.

Uses

Library staff use different tools for bibliographic verification. Some library staff rely on trade directories such as *Global books in print*, others use websites like *BookFinder,* while others may also use a range of publishers' and suppliers' websites.

Trade directories show the resources that have been published and are available for sale. Trade directories provide basic purchasing data. Therefore, trade directories are useful to find:
- if an item is available and how much it costs
- the publisher who published it
- where it can be purchased
- resources on a particular subject.

Be aware, however, that the details found in trade directories should not be treated as authoritative. Trade directories are produced from information supplied by publishers, who have not necessarily viewed the resource. Their information may not conform to library cataloging standards.

Since trade directories include 'in print' resources, irrespective of the date of publication, they are a good place to start if you don't know the date of publication of a resource.

The major caution with trade bibliographies is that they should only be used as alerting tools, and never as the sole means of selecting resources.

EXERCISE 8.7

Choose examples of trade directories in print or electronic form from the list below or from works you find on your own. Fill in the details for five titles. Try to choose some titles from each group.

- *American book publishing record annual*
- *American book trade directory*
- *American reference books annual* (print version) / *ARBAonline* (subscription access) http://www.arbaonline.com/
- *AV market place: the complete business directory of products and services for the audio/video industry*
- *BookFinder* http://www.bookfinder.com/
- *Books in print* (available in print or online by subscription) http://www.bowker.com/products/Books-In--Print.html—any title, e.g.,
    - *Canadian books in print*
    - *Global edition*—contains US, UK, Canadian, European, and Australian publications
    - *United States edition*—contains US publications
    - *Subject guide to Books in print*
- *Book prices current* http://www.bookpricescurrent.com/
- *Bookman's price index: a guide to the values of rare and other out of print books*
- *Directory of library automation software, systems, and services*
- *Fulltext sources online*
- *International directory of little magazines & small presses*
- *Key guide to electronic resources* – any title e.g.,
    - *Key guide to electronic resources: Art and art history*
    - *Key guide to electronic resources: Language and literature*
- *National directory of magazines*
- *Oxbridge directory of newsletters*
- *Standard periodical directory*
- *E-serials : publishers, libraries, users, and standards*

1. Title

   Publisher, copyright date, last updated

   Intended user group

   Arrangement or search options

   Special features

2. Title

   Publisher, copyright date, last updated

   Intended user group

   Arrangement or search options

   Special features

3. Title

   Publisher, copyright date, last updated

   Intended user group

   Arrangement or search options

   Special features

4. Title

   Publisher, copyright date, last updated

   Intended user group

   Arrangement or search options

   Special features

CHAPTER EIGHT   Organizational, Biographical and Trade Directories   111

5. Title

   Publisher, copyright date, last updated

   Intended user group

   Arrangement or search options

   Special features

112 LEARN REFERENCE WORK

EXERCISE 8.8

Find the answer to these questions using a trade directory. Name the source.

1. Name the current resources on photography that are recommended for inclusion in a reference collection.

2. What is the ISSN for *Simple cooking?*

3. What is the current price of *Stockdale's edition of Shakespeare: including in one volume, the whole of his dramatic works*?

4. Who publishes the journal *Oracle story?*

5. Who wrote *The nightingale* that has the ISBN 978-0-312-57722-3?

6. Where could I find details about current architecture periodicals published in the United States and Canada?

7. Name three playwriting and scriptwriting awards that are available for writers.

8. Which online service hosts *American journal of family therapy?*

9. What is the title of the book with the ISBN 978-1-118-73906-8?

10. I want to find book retailers and antiquarians in Toronto and their contact details.

CHAPTER NINE
Yearbooks, Handbooks, Almanacs and Manuals

Introduction
Yearbooks, handbooks, almanacs and manuals are 'fast fact' resources that contain miscellaneous facts and statistics on a variety of topics. They are used to answer ready reference questions. They frequently duplicate information found elsewhere, but their arrangement facilitates speedy access to the information.

These 'fast fact' resources are kept in varying sections of the reference collection. Yearbooks may be classified by subject if they are specific; with the original work if they are updates; or with general almanacs if they are generic. Technically, an almanac is a type of yearbook. General almanacs are classified in 000s (Dewey Decimal Classification) or AY (Library of Congress Classification). Handbooks and manuals are most often subject-specific and are classified by the subject they address.

Characteristics
'Fast fact' resources are revised frequently to ensure the information is up-to-date. They are usually treated as serials in a library, with the latest issue located in the reference collection. Although they vary in layout and content, most have the following in common:
- information is presented in abbreviated form
- there is an emphasis on statistical information
- the arrangement reflects the specific purpose and intended use. It may be alphabetical, chronological or topical
- extensive indexes enhance the resource.

Yearbooks
A yearbook is an annual publication containing current information in brief, descriptive and/or statistical form. Types of yearbooks include:
- **encyclopedia supplements**—published once a year to update the main body of the encyclopedia
- **general yearbooks**—including almanacs, providing miscellaneous facts, e.g., *Whitaker's almanack*, *World almanac*
- **official yearbooks**—published by the government of a country, e.g., *Statistical abstract of the United States*, *South Africa yearbook*
- **yearbooks with subject area summaries**—indicating recent developments, e.g., *Yearbook of technology and education*, *Europa world year book*
- **profession-specific yearbooks**—for a particular trade or profession, e.g., *IMIA yearbook of medical informatics*, *Actors and performers yearbook*

- **statistical yearbooks**—relating to one or more countries, e.g., *Statesman's yearbook, Demographic yearbook, Statistical yearbook for Asia and the Pacific*. The tables of statistics often cover a longer timespan than one year, and are useful for making comparisons.

Handbooks

A handbook is a concise ready reference source of information for a particular field of knowledge. Handbooks treat broad subjects in a brief fashion and may be a useful source of information about a field of knowledge such as science, or an occupational area such as librarianship. They may contain quick facts, tables, statistical information, and perhaps lists of organizations associated with the subject. Examples include *The Law handbook, Handbook of occupational hygiene, Barron's finance and investment handbook, Occupational outlook handbook, Physicians' desk reference*.

Almanacs

An almanac is an annual calendar with astronomical information and other data—a miscellany of useful facts and statistical information. Originally almanacs contained calendars of the months and days including special dates and anniversaries, forecasts of weather and astronomical calculations. They now include more miscellaneous facts, and may cover similar subjects to yearbooks.

Almanacs compress a wealth of facts and figures, both current and retrospective, into one volume. Information is often presented in condensed form in lists or tables. The more detailed almanacs include citations to the original sources, and some may include longer, signed articles covering particularly newsworthy developments such as wars and elections. Examples include *Whitaker's almanack, Australian sports almanac, Canadian almanac and directory, The world almanac and book of facts, The library and book trade almanac*.

Manuals

A manual is a book of instruction on doing, making or performing something. Manuals provide detailed information about rules or procedures, or the operation and maintenance of a product. They cover a wide range of subjects including first aid, car maintenance, or how to run meetings. Examples include *Diagnostic and statistical manual of mental disorders, Roberts rules of order* (a manual of parliamentary procedure), *Chicago manual of style*, the series of *Barron's complete pet owner's manuals*.

Other Sources of Fast Facts
News Summaries

News summaries are daily, weekly or monthly digests of news events. Print versions are loose-leaf in format, designed for storage in binders in chronological order. These summaries are updated and cumulated at regular intervals and include detailed indexes. Most are also available online. Examples include *Facts on file* and *Keesing's record of world events*. By providing access to the date of an event such as a major earthquake or the death of a noteworthy person, news articles can be found in any paper covering the event.

CHAPTER NINE Yearbooks, Handbooks, Almanacs and Manuals

Miscellaneous Tools

Other resources used for ready reference questions include:

- *Chase's calendar of events*—facts and events arranged by calendar date
- *Consumer reports*—buying guide; monthly subscription
- *Emily Post's etiquette*—manners, customs, acceptable behavior
- *Guinness world records*—records of natural and human phenomena
- *Kelley blue book*—pricing for new and used cars (online at http://www.kbb.com)

EXERCISE 9.1

Choose examples of yearbooks, handbooks, almanacs and manuals from the list below or from works you find on your own. Fill in the details for five titles. Try to choose some titles from each type of fast fact reference tool.

Yearbooks

- *Europa world year book / Europa world* (online version http://europaworld.com)
- *Europa regional surveys of the world* (any region, e.g., *The Far East and Australasia* or *Africa south of the Sahara*)
- *Statesman's yearbook* (print or online)
- *World trade annual* (print or online)

Handbooks

- *Parliamentary handbook of the Commonwealth of Australia*
- *Canadian parliamentary handbook*
- *Occupational outlook handbook* (http://www.bls.gov/ooh/home.htm#)
- *SAGE handbook of globalization*
- *The handbook of humanistic psychology*
- *Marks standard handbook for mechanical engineers*
- *CRC handbook of chemistry and physics* (print or online)

Almanacs

- *Library and book trade almanac*
- *Canadian almanac and directory*
- CIA *World factbook*
- *Old farmer's almanac*
- *Information please almanac* or *Time almanac with Information please*
- *Whitaker's almanack* or *Whitaker's concise almanack*
- *The world almanac and book of facts*

Manuals

- Any style manual, e.g.,
  - *Chicago manual of style* (print or online)
  - *Publication manual of the American Psychological Association*, 6th edition
  - the Australian *Style manual for authors, editors and printers*, 6th edition revised by Snooks & Co.

- *Emily Post's etiquette*
- *The Merck manual of medical information*

Miscellaneous Tools
- *Guinness world records* (previously titled *Guinness book of records* and *Guinness book of world records,* online at http://www.guinnessworldrecords.com/)
- *The international book of days*
- *Famous first facts*

1. Title

   Publisher, copyright date, last updated

   Intended user group

   Arrangement or search options

   Special features

2. Title

   Publisher, copyright date, last updated

   Intended user group

   Arrangement or search options

   Special features

CHAPTER NINE Yearbooks, Handbooks, Almanacs and Manuals   117

3. Title

    Publisher, copyright date, last updated

    Intended user group

    Arrangement or search options

    Special features

4. Title

    Publisher, copyright date, last updated

    Intended user group

    Arrangement or search options

    Special features

5. Title

   Publisher, copyright date, last updated

   Intended user group

   Arrangement or search options

   Special features

EXERCISE 9.2

*Suggest a **type** of yearbook, handbook, almanac or manual (e.g., an international statistical yearbook) likely to provide the answers to the following questions. You do not have to answer the questions, or give an exact title or bibliographic details for the type of tool.*

1. How many dentists are there in the United States?

2. Where can I find names of the current administration of Honduras?

3. What are the functions of the World Health Organization?

4. Where can I find information about repairing the engine of a Ford Focus?

5. Has the birth rate of Ireland gone up or down in the past five years?

6. I need a list of major Greek and Roman gods and goddesses of the classical world. Where can I find it?

7. Where would I find advice on how to use gender-inclusive language?

8. Who was the King of England in 1770?

9. Which countries import orange juice? How much do they import and what is the value in US dollars?

10. I'd like an overview of international organizations. Where can I find one?

EXERCISE 9.3

Find the answer to these questions using a yearbook, handbook, almanac or manual. Name the source.

1. Where can I find the national holidays of Germany for the next calendar year?

2. Where would I find information on the history of Tonga?

3. Is Kakadu National Park a World Heritage site?

4. What is the address of the Indonesia Tourist Promotion Board?

5. When should I use an apostrophe when writing a report?

6. Where would I find a list of the world's longest bridges?

7. What minerals are produced in Ethiopia?

8. Who invented the Ferris wheel and when was it first erected?

9. Where can I find a list of the 'Best Books for Young Adults'?

10. I need a list of Academy Award winning movies and actors for the past five years. Where can I find that information?

CHAPTER TEN
Geographic Tools

Introduction
There are a number of geographical resources available to assist with reference queries about places. Unlike other types of reference tools, which are usually print resources or their online equivalent, geographical resources come in a variety of formats. They include atlases, maps, globes, gazetteers and guidebooks.

Geographical Resources
Atlases, maps, globes, gazetteers and guidebooks are reference tools that provide visual and written details of countries, cities, landforms, oceans and waterways. They can also include material on climate, population and statistical information.

Geographical resources are classed in Dewey Decimal Classification 910, and in Library of Congress Classification 'G'. While atlases, gazetteers and current guidebooks are usually kept in the reference collection, older guidebooks are often moved to the general collection. Maps are usually housed separately in special map cabinets.

Characteristics
Geographic reference tools present spatial information in a variety of formats. Maps are created by cartographers (mapmakers). Atlases and gazetteers are compiled by geographers and geoscientists. Guidebooks are prepared either by professional travel writers or with contributions from laymen. In all cases, frequent updating is needed to reflect political, economic and environmental changes.

A basic understanding of concepts related to maps and atlases is helpful when dealing with spatial resources. Useful terms include:
- **cartouche**—the equivalent of a title page for a map; the ornamental frame includes the title of the map, name of cartographer, scale, date and other descriptive elements
- **globe**—a spherical representation of the earth or another celestial body
- **grid**—the set of lines that show coordinates on a map, often showing latitude and longitude
- **latitude and longitude**—imaginary lines established by convention to represent places on earth, described in degrees, minutes and seconds north, south, east or west of agreed baselines
- **legend or key**—an explanation of the symbols used on a map
- **projection**—the mathematical formula allowing a flat representation of a spherical surface. There is always some distortion on a flat map
- **scale**—the relationship between distance on a map and actual distance on the earth. Scale may be represented by words (e.g., 'one inch equals one mile') or a ratio (e.g., '1:63,360')

Maps and atlases are not limited to the planet earth—they can depict all parts of the solar system.

Uses
Geographic reference tools are used to answer a range of place-related queries. They can assist with:
- maps of a specific area or on a specific topic—e.g., vegetation, minerals, population
- current or historical information on a specific subject—e.g., old landfill sites
- details of places and place names (including approved names and spellings, used by catalogers)
- information about major features or attractions of countries or cities
- interpretation of information—e.g., "Was the 'Silk Road' one route or many?"

Types of Geographic Reference Tools
- **maps and charts**—portray elements of the three-dimensional world on a two-dimensional surface. There are many types of maps including physical, thematic (i.e., dealing with specific subjects), political and economic. Maps can be printed or digital. Maps can be stand-alone, or part of a series where each sheet is produced to a standard format and abuts its neighbour to form a larger whole. Series maps are accessed using an *index map* that shows the larger whole overlaid with the names and/or numbers of the separate sheets in the series.
- **online digital and interactive maps**—maps in digital form, to be viewed and/or printed from online sources. These are often street maps used for locational and directional information—e.g., *Google maps* (https://www.google.com/maps); *whereis* (http://www.whereis.com), etc. Many incorporate image-based systems using aerial photography and satellite imagery to show bird's-eye views or multiple angles of locations. Interactive maps allow users to create their own maps, often using GIS systems and overlaying information from available data sets.
- **atlases**—a collection of maps, usually in book form. Atlases include place name indexes (similar to but not as detailed as a gazetteer) to help locate information on individual maps, and may include related information presented as smaller ancillary maps, charts or statistics. Types of atlases include international, national, regional, economic, historical, thematic (i.e., on a particular topic), and road or street directories.
- **GIS (Geographic Information Systems)**—sophisticated mapping tools used to create maps and manipulate spatial data. Maps produced by GIS differ from traditional maps by being digital rather than analog. They are made up of differing layers of data depending on purpose, e.g., fire route maps layering streets, postal codes, and fire hydrant locations. These maps are the basis of navigation systems now used in automobiles.
- **gazetteers**—geographical dictionaries listing places and their locations. Gazetteers provide factual information about places. Recent editions describe the place as it is now, and older editions provide historical information. Entries in a gazetteer may include pronunciation, location, area, population, geographical and physical description and historical data. They can be in print or online form.

- **geographic names records**—similar to gazetteers, but focusing on the approved forms of names for various regions and features, and/or the origins of the names. The Library of Congress web page http://www.lcweb.loc.gov/catdir/cpso/geogname.html provides information about accessing online tools for American and international geographic names. City government offices and local councils have records for the names of streets and parks. Books devoted to place names for specific countries, provinces, states or regions may give more detail regarding the names of local streets, parks, schools, and other features.
- **guidebooks and travel guides**—print or online resources that provide brief historical information about a particular place as well as detailed descriptions of hotels, museums, restaurants, famous sites and other information useful to travelers. Some publishers like Fodors and Lonely Planet specialize in print and online travel guides. A large number of online travel guides are produced by government tourist agencies at the country, state, province or local level, to promote their regions. In addition, there are many web-based travel sites like *Virtual Tourist* (https://www.virtualtourist.com) and *Trip Advisor* (https://www.tripadvisor.com) that focus on feedback from travelers.

Evaluating Geographic Tools

When deciding on a geographic tool to acquire or to use in answering a query, consider the following:
- **accuracy**—national boundaries and place names should be accurate, but this information can become out of date very quickly, particularly in printed materials
- **uniform treatment of place names**—there may be a problem transliterating non-Roman alphabets. Many atlases and gazetteers follow patterns established by standards bodies
- **balance of coverage**—a world atlas may give the most emphasis to maps of the country of publication
- **authority of the publisher**—is the publishing body the organization that created the maps, or a third-party onseller? Are the publishers experienced in dealing with maps and atlases?
- **currency**—information should be up-to-date and updated regularly
- **ease of use**—does the resource include instructions on use? Does it include explanations of map symbols and projections used? Is it easy to read or to navigate?
- **color and scale**—if the resource is a map, is it in color and does the color assist with interpreting the map? Is the scale appropriate to the information being portrayed?
- **additional information**—does the source provide a comprehensive index? Are there extra features such as tables showing the longest rivers in the world or the highest mountains?

Other Sources of Geographical Information

Although maps, gazetteers and atlases are the traditional sources of geographical information, the following are also useful:
- *encyclopedias* describe countries and places, and include maps of particular areas
- *yearbooks* indicate name and boundary changes
- *dictionaries* provide brief identification of larger places and pronunciation of geographical terms and place names
- *biographical dictionaries* give information on geographers and cartographers
- *bibliographies and carto-bibliographies* have details of books containing geographical information; or lists of maps giving descriptive information
- *periodical indexes* include articles on geographical topics
- *census data* include maps and other geographical information to illustrate the data
- *statistical sources* provide geographical information in tabular form.

Political, economic and environmental changes frequently require information to be updated. Therefore it is very important to check the currency of these sources.

Some reference tools are not created specifically for locational information, but their focus and arrangement make them useful for answering geographical reference queries. For example:
- The CIA *World factbook* http://www.cia.gov/library/publications/the-world-factbook/ is an online resource that provides information on the history, people, government, economy, geography, communications, transportation, military, and transnational issues for 267 world entities. It includes maps of the major world regions, as well as physical, political, standard time zone and world oceans maps. It can be used to answer questions like: where is the largest freshwater lake in Central America; which countries are members of Interpol; what country's capital is Nuku'alofa; which Polynesian nation owns the Internet domain extension '.tv'; the size of any country compared to the United States; the total land border length for any country, etc.
- The United States Census Bureau website has a section on maps and data http://www.census.gov/geo/maps-data/ where users can view and print county demographic and landform maps, thematic maps (demographic, economic, business or socioeconomic), cartographic boundary files, gazetteer files, and name look-up tables for entities from the census
- The Australian Geoscience Information Network (AUSGIN) portal http://www.geoscience.gov.au is designed as a single point of access to geological and geophysical data for mineral exploration in Australia, and also provides access to the 1:250,000 Geological Map series of Australia, the *Australian Mine Atlas*, and a number of online GIS mapping systems.

EXERCISE 10.1

Choose examples of geographic tools in print or electronic form from the list below or from works you find on your own. Fill in the details for five titles. Try to choose some titles from each group.

Atlases
- *Times comprehensive atlas of the world* (or any general print atlas)
- *National Geographic concise atlas of the world* (or any student atlas)
- *The atlas of Canada* http://www.nrcan.gc.ca/earth-sciences/geography/atlas-canada, or the *Atlas South Australia* http://www.atlas.sa.gov.au/, or any online regional atlas
- Any road atlas or street directory
- *Owl and Mouse online atlas* http://www.yourchildlearns.com/online-atlas.htm, or any print atlas for children
- Any thematic atlas (on a topic or subject), e.g., an historical atlas, an atlas of religion, an atlas of mineral or natural resources, etc.—print or online

Gazetteers
- Any print gazetteer in your library
- *Gazetteer of Australia* http://www.ga.gov.au/place-names/index.xhtml
- *Gazetteer of planetary nomenclature* http://planetarynames.wr.usgs.gov/
- *Getty thesaurus of geographic names* http://www.getty.edu/research/tools/vocabularies/tgn/index.html/
- *JewishGen gazetteer* http://www.jewishgen.org/Communities/About.htm
- *United States Board on Geographic Names* http://geonames.usgs.gov/
- *Columbia gazetteer of the world* (by subscription only, if you can access from your library) http://www.columbiagazetteer.org/main/Home.page

Digital interactive or online maps
- *NatureMaps (South Australia)* https://data.environment.sa.gov.au/NatureMaps/Pages/default.aspx
- National Geographic *MapMaker Interactive* http://education.nationalgeographic.org/mapping/
- World Health Organization *Global atlas of infectious diseases* http://gamapserver.who.int/GlobalAtlas/home.asp
- *Mappery* http://www.mappery.com/about.php
- *Maproom* http://www.maproom.org/
- *Atlas of living Australia* http://www.ala.org.au/

Guidebooks or travel guides *(or others found in your library)*
- *Lonely planet*—any print title, for any place
- *Fodor's guides*—any print title, for any place
- *TripAdvisor* website http://www.tripadvisor.com—choose any place
- *Virtual tourist* website http://www.virtualtourist.com/—choose any place

1. Title

    Publisher, copyright date, last updated

    Intended user group

    Arrangement or search options

    Special features

2. Title

    Publisher, copyright date, last updated

    Intended user group

    Arrangement or search options

    Special features

3. Title

>   Publisher, copyright date, last updated

>   Intended user group

>   Arrangement or search options

>   Special features

4. Title

>   Publisher, copyright date, last updated

>   Intended user group

>   Arrangement or search options

>   Special features

5. Title

>Publisher, copyright date, last updated

>Intended user group

>Arrangement or search options

>Special features

EXERCISE 10.2

*Suggest a **type** of geographic tool (e.g., a thematic atlas) likely to provide the answers to the following questions. You do not have to answer the questions, or give an exact title or bibliographic details for the geographic tool.*

1. A library user wants visual directions to the local museum.

2. A teacher is looking for maps to show the rivers and lakes in western Europe.

3. A theology lecturer needs a map illustrating the religions of the world.

4. A student needs to identify specific constellations for an astronomy project.

5. A library patron is looking for a map showing the battles of the American Civil War.

6. A family historian is trying to locate a village in Germany where his ancestors originated.

7. A health researcher wants to show where the hospitals are located in relation to the area's aged care homes.

8. A student needs to compare the elevations of Denver, Colorado and Mexico City.

9. A grandmother wants to know the origin of the name of the town where she was born.

10. A library user is trying to locate information on Paris to plan a trip.

EXERCISE 10.3

Using a gazetteer or atlas from the reference collection, find the country in which the following places are located. Note that you may need to use more than one source.

1. Parana

2. Fairborn

3. Storvik

4. Strasbourg

5. Malaut

6. Engan

7. Benevento

8. Minyip

9. Mobara

10. Mary's Harbour

CHAPTER ELEVEN
Government Documents

Introduction

The previous chapters looked at types of reference tools based on their format (dictionaries, directories, manuals, etc.) In this chapter we examine a range of tools covering many of these formats, whose common theme is their source: they have all been created and published by governments.

Government documents (also referred to as *government publications*) are useful reference tools because of the authoritative nature of their source, as well as their content. They provide information frequently not available in other publications, and are therefore unique sources of information. Government publications are produced by a wide range of bodies including legislatures, judiciary, statutory authorities and boards of inquiry. Every country produces government reports and documents at the whole-of-country level. States, provinces and local governments also produce documents that are important for libraries.

In order to effectively find information from government sources, it is useful to have a basic understanding of the structure of government in that country. For example, most democracies have three distinct branches of government: the Executive (or Presidency, or Monarchy/representative of monarch), the Congress or Parliament, and the Judiciary. Many parliaments have two parts, or 'houses': in the USA these are the House of Representatives and the Senate; in Great Britain the House of Commons and the House of Lords; in Canada the House of Commons and the Senate; in Australia the House of Representatives and the Senate, and so on. The functions and responsibilities of the houses may differ in various countries. Knowing the names of the parts of government, and what roles they play, will assist in understanding who produces government documents, and for what purpose.

This chapter examines the government documents of the United States, Canada and Australia. It also briefly addresses publications from their states, provinces and local governments. Depending on your country of residence, you may wish to focus specifically on relevant sections of this chapter; however, you should ensure you also have a good overview of the publications of the other jurisdictions.

United States Government Documents

The United States Government Publishing Office (formerly the U.S. Government Printing Office, or GPO) has been described as the largest publisher in the world. U.S. government documents can be cataloged by libraries and classified using Library of Congress or Dewey Decimal classification. However, libraries with large collections of federal documents generally use the classification system of the Superintendent of Documents (SuDocs). This classification system was developed over several years from 1895 to 1903 and was issued by the Superintendent of Documents in 1904. It is designed to organize publications by government author or agency.

The Superintendent of Documents (SuDocs) Classification System arranges materials by issuing agency, not by subject. The table below shows the general class breakdown. See http://www.fdlp.gov/catalogingandclassification/cataloging-articles/1791-sudocs-classification?showall=1&limitstart= for a more detailed explanation.

Agency	Code	Agency	Code
Agriculture Department	A	National Archives and Records Administration	AE
Broadcasting Board of Governors	B	Commerce Department	C
Federal Communications Commission	CC	Civil Rights Commission	CR
Defense Department	D	Energy Department	E
Education Department	ED	Environmental Protection Agency	EP
Fine Arts Commission	FA	Farm Credit Administration	FCA
Federal Housing Financing Board	FHF	Federal Mediation and Conciliation Service	FM
Federal Maritime Commission	FMC	Federal Reserve System Board of Governors	FR
Federal Trade Commission	FT	Foreign-Trade Zones Board	FTZ
Government Accountability Office	GA	Government Printing Office	GP
General Services Administration	GS	Health and Human Services Department	HE
Housing and Urban Development Department	HH	Homeland Security	HS
Interior Department	I	Interstate Commerce Commission	IC
US Agency for International Development	ID	International Trade Commission	ITC
Justice Department	J	Judiciary	JU
Labor Department	L	Library of Congress	LC
National Labor Relations Board	LR	Merit Systems Protection Board	MS
National Aeronautics and Space Administration	NAS	National Capital Planning Commission	NC
National Credit Union Administration	NCU	National Foundation on the Arts and the Humanities	NF
National Mediation Board	NMB	National Science Foundation	NS
Overseas Private Investment Corporation	OP	United States Postal Service	P
Peace Corps	PE	Personnel Management Office	PM
President of the United States	PR	Executive Office of the President	PREX
Vice President of the United States	PRVP	Railroad Retirement Board	RR
State Department	S	Small Business Administration	SBA
Securities and Exchange Commission	SE	Smithsonian Institution	SI
Social Security Administration	SSA	Treasury Department	T
Transportation Department	TD	US Trade and Development Agency	TDA
Veterans Affairs Department	VA	Congress	X, Y

CHAPTER ELEVEN Government Documents 133

> **EXERCISE 11.1**
> *Using the information provided above, identify which agency issued the documents that have been assigned the following SuDocs numbers:*

1. C 3.24/8:IN23

2. NAS 1.2:FR 76

3. NS 1.53:990k

4. D 1.2:EX83

5. I 29.6/4t

6. SI 1.1/A:AE82/5

7. A 67.7/3:11/5

8. ED 1.109

9. Y 4.P93/1:1P/

10. PREX

SuDocs Number

A SuDocs number consists of a class number and a book number. It is written using letters, numbers, and one or more separators (slashes, colons and periods). When the date is included in the book number, the year is often abbreviated by dropping the first number—e.g., 986 for 1986 (the publication date).

A SuDocs number may include:
- the source of the document (mandatory)
- the type of document (circular, serial, etc.)
- serial details (volume, issue, etc.)
- whether it is part of a series
- the date of publication.

SuDoc call numbers may be written vertically or horizontally:

    I 29.6/4: B86/986   or   I 29
                                        6/4
                                        B86/986

 To find an item using its SuDocs number, it is helpful to recognize the various parts of the number. Here is an example:

                      I 29.6/4: B86/986
                class number: book/item number

In the number above:
- I = Interior Department (issuing agency)
- 29 = National Park Service (section of the issuing agency)
- 6 = National Parks Information Circulars (type of document)
- 4 = National Rivers, Information Circulars (more specific type of document)
- B = Buffalo (first word of title)
- 86 = *Buffalo National River: official map and guide* (specific title)
- 986 = 1986 (publication date)

Availability of U.S. Federal Documents

The Federal Depository Libraries program ensures that U.S. federal government documents are available to the public through various libraries. Federal depository libraries are located in every state. More than 1,500 libraries receive documents, at no charge, according to a specific profile. Public, university, college, or special libraries may become depository libraries. Most depository libraries are selective, and receive only documents in particular categories. There are at least two depository libraries in each congressional district. In addition, about 50 regional depository libraries receive all materials available for deposit. Documents in federal depository libraries are accessible to all U.S. citizens.

Government documents are produced in various formats including paper, CD-ROM, microfiche, and online. A growing number of current documents are available online and accessed through FDsys, the Federal Digital System of the Government Publishing Office, at https://www.gpo.gov/fdsys/search/home.action.

Selected U.S. Government Document Tools

U.S. government documents are free of copyright so some information is also available from commercial publishers such as ProQuest, Congressional Quarterly Press (CQ), Bernan, and others. These publishers repackage the information with 'value added' features, easier access and/or indexing. With the de-funding of many government publishing programs in the early 2010s, publishing of government data by commercial services has increased.

Federal documents are available in all types of reference tools. There are also many commercially produced tools to assist in sourcing U.S. documents. Some have been mentioned in earlier chapters as important resources for reference work. Major titles (with their SuDoc numbers) may be repeated here. Many are available via the Internet.

Fast Facts and Statistical Information
Statistical abstract of the United States is one of the most widely used reference tools for U.S. statistical data. It was produced annually by the Census Bureau until 2011, when the government terminated funding for the compilation of the data. The commercial publisher ProQuest now compiles and produces the publication. *Statistical abstract of the United States* is often found in ready reference collections. The print and electronic versions include popular statistical data from all federal agencies as well as from non-government sources. It is complemented by other commercial publications such as the *World almanack* and the *Europa world yearbook*, and by ProQuest's suite of statistical databases covering federal, state, business and international statistical publications.

The United States takes a census at the beginning of every decade. Census information is available via the Internet and in many depository libraries. The *Statistical abstract of the United States* also provides a great deal of concise statistical information from the census. General demographic information is available soon after the completion of the census; details of individual persons are only released 72 years after the census. *United States Census Bureau* is available online at http://www.census.gov/.

Like *Statistical abstract*, some key crime statistical publications were de-funded by the U.S. government in the early 2010s. However, *Crime in the United States*, also known as *Uniform crime reports*, (J 1.14/7-8) (http://www.fbi.gov/about-us/cjis/ucr/ucr-publications) is one of a number of publications the Federal Bureau of Investigation still produces. These supplement a range of statistical publications from the Bureau of Justice Statistics (BJS), (http://www.bjs.gov/).

The *Fast facts* webpage of the National Center for Education Statistics (NCES) website (http://nces.ed.gov/), provides concise statistical information on educational issues from early childhood to adult learning. Additional references are given with each fact. The NCES website links several major U.S. Department of Education publications including the *Digest of educational statistics* (K-12 and postsecondary education), the *Condition of education* (ED 1.109) and *Projections of education statistics*.

Handbooks, Manuals, and Yearbooks
United States government manual (http://www.gpoaccess.gov/manual/) is the official handbook of the federal government. The *Manual* (AE 2.108/) is published annually and provides a description, mission statement, and relationships or reporting lines for agencies and offices. Names and contact information for key personnel are also included. Since 2011 the *Manual* has been freely available online through the FDsys Federal Digital System.

The Standard industrial classification (SIC) code was used for many years to provide a numeric symbol for aspects of industries. The Code was sponsored by the Office of Management and Budget (OMB). In 1997 the NAICS codes replaced the SIC codes for mostpurposes. NAICS—North American industry classification system is sponsored by the Bureau of Census. The use of the codes is essential in business research.

Other handbooks of note include:
- *Occupational outlook handbook* from the Bureau of Labor Statistics, describing careers (GP 3.22/2:270/)
- *World factbook* from the Central Intelligence Agency (CIA) (PREX 3.15) http://www.cia.gov/library/publications/resources/the-world-factbook/index.html

Biographical Resources
- *Official congressional directory* (Y 4.P93/1:1/) is a very valuable source. Published for each term of Congress (i.e., every two years), it contains information about each of the senators and representatives of the Congress, including their biographical information and official committee appointments. It is available online at http://www.gpo.gov/fdsys/browse/collection.action?collectionCode=CDIR
- *Congressional pictorial directory* (Y 4.P93/1:1P/) provides pictures of the President, Vice President, each member of the House of Representatives and the Senate and House and Senate officers and officials for each term of Congress.

Geographical Information
The United States Geological Survey (USGS) https://www.usgs.gov produces thousands of maps and provides an invaluable resource for map collections. Maps in digital format, geographical data layers and place name information are also publications of USGS. In addition, the USGS Publications Warehouse https://pubs.er.usgs.gov provides access to over 130,000 publications written by USGS scientists over the last 200 years, including journal articles, series reports, book chapters, other government publications and conference proceedings.

Bibliographies
The major finding tool for U.S. government publications is the *Catalog of U.S. government publications* http://catalog.gpo.gov/. It covers historical and current publications and provides direct links to publications in electronic format when available. It can be searched by authoring agency, title, subject and keyword. This online catalog incorporates the former printed *Monthly catalog of United States government publications*.

Directories
Several directories stand out as important sources for reference work:
- *Official congressional directory,* mentioned above, is a directory for and about Congress. Brief biographies are provided for each senator and representative along with contact information, and committee assignments. This tool is heavily used.
- *Washington information directory,* a commercially produced publication in print and online, provides information from the *Congressional directory* and the *U.S. government manual* but also includes non-government groups like foundations, lobbying organizations, and associations.
- *Zip code directory* from the United States Postal Service provides a free online lookup tool and is a useful ready reference resource for many libraries https://www.usps.com/nationalpremieraccounts/findzipcodes.htm.

Indexes and Abstracts

The United States is served by five libraries that act as national collections in their subject areas. Their bibliographic databases are the basis for major indexing and abstracting services. Some of these are publicly accessible via the Internet, others are available through commercial publishers like Ebsco and ProQuest.

AGRICOLA http://agricola.nal.usda.gov/, created by the National Agricultural Library, is a catalog and database index to the largest agricultural library collection in the world. The index includes monographs and journal articles in the areas of agriculture, plant and animal sciences, forestry, entomology and others.

ERIC (Educational resources information center) (http://www.eric.ed.gov/) was established in 1960 to handle education materials. Today it is an Internet-based digital library of education research and information sponsored by the Institute of Education Sciences (IES) of the U.S. Department of Education. ERIC provides access to bibliographic records of journal and non-journal literature indexed from 1966 to the present.

MEDLINE, from the National Library of Medicine (NLM), is the standard index to medical literature. The paper equivalent is *IndexMedicus.* The free public access version, *PubMed,* (http://www.ncbi.nlm.nih.gov/pubmed) contains some links to current full-text articles. *PubMed Central* is a free full-text archive of the Library's journal articles. *MEDLINE* is also available through several commercial vendors. The differences are in the software provided.

Legislative and Judicial Information

Congress.gov (https://www.congress.gov/) is the official website for U.S. federal legislative information. It is produced by the Library of Congress and provides links to various sources of information on legislative government. *Congress.gov* replaced an earlier website, *Thomas.gov* (named for Thomas Jefferson), in 2016. The site covers data from both houses of Congress, the Government Publishing Office, Congressional Budget Office and the Library of Congress' Congressional Research Service.

The U.S. Department of Justice website (http://www.justice.gov) contains a variety of resources including publications, reports, case highlights, and the history of a range of legislation. Its 'Agencies' page (https://www.justice.gov/agencies) links to the websites of 60 agencies, each of which provide their reports and publications. The website's 'Justice 101' page (https://www.justice.gov/usao/justice-101/federal-courts) gives an overview of the federal court system. More detailed information about the U.S. judicial system can be found on the *United States Courts* website http://www.uscourts.gov

U.S. State and Local Documents

U.S. state and local governments generally have websites. *GovEngine.com* provides links to local government websites for counties, municipalities and townships in each state at http://www.govengine.com/localgov/index.html. Documents not available electronically from the websites can often be located through a local library.

EXERCISE 11.2

Indicate the U.S. government document where you would expect to find information on the following topics:

1. Biographical information about the senators representing any U.S. state.

2. Statistics regarding violent crime in any U.S. state.

3. Ordering information for a specific document.

4. Periodical articles on agriculture.

5. Demographics of a U.S. city of your choice.

6. Legislative information on a current bill.

7. A photograph of the Vice-President.

8. Sample curriculum for third grade mathematics courses.

9. Current information about childhood cancer.

10. Information about Cuba.

EXERCISE 11.3

Look at the following U.S. Government Internet sites and suggest a question that might be answered from each site:

1. Statistical Abstract of the United States
   http://www.census.gov/library/publications/time-series/statistical_abstracts.html

2. Bureau of Justice Statistics
   http://www.bjs.gov/

3. United States Government Manual
   http://www.gpo.gov/fdsys/browse/collection.action?collectionCode=GOVMAN

4. Congress.gov
   http://www.congress.gov/

5. U.S. Census Bureau
   http://www.census.gov/

Canadian Government Documents

Since 2013, the government of Canada has been transitioning from primarily print-based documents, published by the now-disbanded Canadian Government Publishing (CGP), to electronic documents published by individual government departments. In 2016, a new *Policy on Communications and Federal Identity* identified digital media and platforms as 'the primary means to interact with the public', and electronic publishing as the standard for Government of Canada publications.

Public Works and Government Services Canada is the department responsible for making government documents readily accessible to the public. Its Publishing and Depository Services (PDS) maintains a central online database of publications authored by the Government of Canada. The *publications.gc.ca* website (http://publications.gc.ca) provides open access to more than 275,000 searchable catalog records, and hosts over 150,000 digital publications, such as research papers, periodicals and monographs. More than 1,000 titles are added to the collection every month.

The documents themselves are maintained by the authoring departments, but Publishing and Depository Services is the central repository for the publications. Older documents that were only published in print form are gradually being digitized; however catalog records for publications that will never be converted to electronic format will continue to appear in the database so that it remains a complete record of government publishing. PDS also administers Crown Copyright and licensing agreements, and assigns ISBN, ISSN and Government of Canada Catalogue Numbers to each departmental publication.

GC Catalogue Numbers

The Canadian Government organizes its publications using an alpha-numeric text string indicating the department, publication type and date of publication. Valid GC Catalogue Numbers are assigned only by PDS. Author departments are not authorized to construct and assign their own GC Catalogue Numbers.

 A GC Catalogue Number typically takes the form **En40-568/2001E**, where:
- initial alphabetic characters identify the issuing department or agency (in this example, Environment Canada)
- the numbers immediately following identify the branch of the department or agency (in this example, 40 represents Environmental Protection)
- the next group of numbers signifies the publication type (annual, monograph, series or periodical) then the series and issue numbers, or the DSP (Depository Services Program) accession number (in this example, this is the 568th Environmental Protection monograph recorded by the DSP)
- the final number indicates the date of publication and the final letter or letters (if present) may indicate the language of the publication (in this example, E indicates English), or the format of the publication if it is not a standard print format publication, or both language and format.

Source: *About Government of Canada Catalogue Numbers*, viewed August 2016, http://publications.gc.ca/site/eng/isbn/aboutCatalogueNumbers.html.

A new GC Catalogue Number is assigned to each new individual publication, including:
- each new annual edition
- each issue in a series
- each new edition or revision
- each separate language edition
- each additional publication format (print, CD-ROM, PDF, etc.)

The GC Catalogue Number is a tracking tool like an ISBN. While it can be used to classify government publication collections, it is not as heavily used for this purpose as, for example, the SuDocs numbers are for United States government documents.

Availability of Canadian Federal Documents

Like the United States, the Government of Canada maintained a Depository Services Program (DSP) from 1927 to 2013. The DSP sent government publications to academic, college, legislative and public libraries in Canada and selected countries. With the transition to an electronic-only publication model, the DSP stopped distributing print publications in early 2014. Now, Publishing and Depository Services acts as the Government of Canada's 'information safety net', by issuing a weekly checklist of the latest government publications as well as its online catalog http://publications.gc.ca/site/eng/ourCatalogue.html.

Government documents can also be accessed via the Government of Canada *Canada.ca* website's 'Publications' page https://www.canada.ca/en/government/publications.html which allows one to search for publications using keywords or catalog numbers, or find publications by federal government department or agency.

EXERCISE 11.4
Use the Canadian Government's online catalog to answer the following questions. Write down your search strategy for each answer:

1. A farmer wants some publications about how the government can help to mediate farm debt.

2. Are there any recent government documents about bees?

3. A teacher asks if the government has produced any material about the Air Quality Health Index for use in education. She particularly wants:

   a) Some titles and/or bibliographic details for any resources

   b) Which department/s produced them

   c) How to obtain copies

4. Has the government produced any publications about Lyme Disease?

Selected Canadian Government Document Tools

Canadian government publications are authored by individual departments and agencies, and as noted above can be accessed through the *publications.ga.ca* site catalog. Another access point is via the *Canada.ca* website (http://www.canada.ca). The website's aim is to eventually merge all federal department and agency websites into one unified website, organized by topics to allow users to find and access government information and services more easily. This task has been undertaken in phases since 2013, and existing federal websites will remain active until their content is fully migrated to the *Canada.ca* site. The *Canada.ca* site is a good first point of call for finding a variety of government document tools.

Statistical Information

Statistics and data from a range of departments and agencies are found via the *Canada.ca* web page https://www.canada.ca/en/government/statistics/dept.html. The page lists each department or agency that produces statistics, and indicates what sort of information can be found on their sites. The extract below shows the format of the page:

> ...
> **Canada Revenue Agency**
> Includes income statistics and GST/HST statistics.
>
> **Canadian Grain Commission**
> Includes information about grain elevators, grain exports, deliveries and other grain-related subjects.
>
> **Canadian Tourism Commission**
> Provides statistical data and information for business owners and CEOs on Canada's world tourism market.
> ...

The most common source of statistical information is Statistics Canada, the country's central statistics-collecting organization. In Canada, providing statistics is a federal responsibility, and Statistics Canada collects and disseminates statistical information on the social, commercial, financial and economic situation in the country as a whole and for each of the provinces and territories. The Statistics Canada website http://www.statcan.gc.ca/eng/start presents data derived from over 350 surveys, covering economic indicators as well as subjects ranging from retail trade to senior citizens.

Statistics Canada is also responsible for administering the country's census. The census provides a statistical portrait of Canada and its people. Statistics Canada administers the Census Program, which is carried out every five years. Since 2011, the Census Program has consisted of two parts: a short questionnaire (census) with a basic set of questions distributed to 100% of households, or a long questionnaire (*National Household Survey*) distributed to a 33% sample of households. A Census of Agriculture is also collected with the Census of Population, covering all farms and agricultural operations. The most recent census was in May 2016. Key statistics, topics, and data sets for recent population censuses are available from the 'Census Program' page of the Statistics Canada website http://www12.statcan.gc.ca/census-recensement/index-eng.cfm?HPA=1. Data sets from the Census of Agriculture can be downloaded from the government's Open Data Portal http://open.canada.ca/data/en/dataset?organization=statcan.

Handbooks, Manuals, and Yearbooks
The *Canada year book* was published annually from 1867 to 2012 by Statistics Canada. Presented in almanac style for ready reference, the publication included tables, charts and analytical articles on every major subject in Statistics Canada's areas of expertise. It has been replaced by online summary tables on individual topics, that are updated monthly or quarterly on the Statistics Canada website. Many libraries use the two products in tandem: accessing the up-to-date tables for current information and referring to the print products for historical or background information.

To supplement its data tables, Statistics Canada also produces an annual publication, *Canada at a glance* http://www.statcan.gc.ca/pub/12-581-x/12-581-x2016000-eng.htm. While it does not include the analytical commentary of the former *Canada year book*, this ready-reference online booklet succinctly presents statistics, charts and tables on key topics like population, education, crime, housing, etc. as well as international comparisons of key economic and demographic indicators.

Biographical Resources
Canadian government biographies index is an unofficial online source for information on a range of Canadians who have served the government. It includes profiles of prime ministers and provincial premiers, and influential public servants and reformers. Biographies are indexed by surname, as well as by the following topics: Prime Ministers of Canada; Canadian Provincial Premiers, Canadian women in government; and Canadian astronauts. While there are some historical figures included, many of the biographies are for contemporary figures. http://canadaonline.about.com/od/canadiansingovernment/a/biographieslist.htm.

Biographical information about currently serving Parliamentarians is available on the *Parliament of Canada* website's PARLINFO pages, using the 'Senate' and 'House of Commons' tags. http://www.lop.parl.gc.ca/ParlInfo/default.aspx?Menu=Home.

Geographical Information
Natural Resources Canada (NRCan) produces thousands of maps and the *Atlas of Canada* online http://www.nrcan.gc.ca/earth-sciences/geography/atlas-canada. These provide a valuable source of geographic information for map collections. Selected thematic maps, interactive maps, digital data and a mapping tool are available.

Statistics Canada produces road, boundary, electoral district, census division, and a range of thematic maps as part of its census geography program. The maps are updated at each census. http://www12.statcan.gc.ca/census-recensement/2011/geo/index-eng.cfm

Since 1897 the Geographic Names Board of Canada has made decisions about names for Canadian maps. It supports the Canadian Geographical Names Database (CGNDB) that allows users to search for information on any place name in Canada. http://www.nrcan.gc.ca/earth-sciences/geography/place-names/search/9170

Bibliographies
The *Government of Canada catalogue* http://publications.gc.ca/site/eng/ourCatalogue.html contains the most comprehensive list of print and electronic government publications. Its *Weekly acquisitions list* (http://publications.gc.ca/site/eng/weeklyAcquisitionList/lists.html) alerts users to new material published.

Directories
The *Government Electronic Directory Services* (GEDS) is a directory listing of public servants in federal government departments and agencies across Canada. Users can search for a specific individual, or browse the organizational hierarchy of a department for staff contact numbers, work addresses and work roles. There are also links to Ministers, Deputy Ministers, Senators and Members of Parliament and their staff. http://www.geds.gc.ca/en/GEDS/?pgid=002.

Each Province and Territory maintains a staff directory on its own website. They are called variously 'government directory', 'staff directory', 'telephone directory', 'contact numbers', 'employee directory', etc. and in most cases can be located via the site's 'Contact Us' page. An unofficial consolidated list of the directories, with a short explanation of what is covered in each, is available at http://canadaonline.about.com/od/govtdirectories/

Indexes and Abstracts
The major index of government documents is a commercial product, ProQuest's *Canadian Research Index* http://www.proquest.com/products-services/canadian_research.html. The *Index* includes bibliographic citations and abstracts for federal, provincial and municipal documents issued by departments and agencies, as well as scientific and technical reports by research institutes and government laboratories. A microfiche service, *Microlog*, provides the full text of the documents described in the *Index*. The *Index* is available in electronic format by subscription and new titles are added monthly.

Legislative and Judicial Information
Information on Parliamentary legislation can be found through *LEGISinfo* (http://www.parl.gc.ca/LEGISInfo/). This is a research tool for locating information on legislation currently before the Canadian Parliament. This tool provides electronic access to a wide range of information about individual bills, such as:
- the text of the bill at various stages
- government press releases and backgrounders (for government bills)
- legislative summaries from the Parliamentary Information and Research Service.

LEGISinfo can display all bills for a Parliamentary session, or filter by originating chamber (Senate or House of Commons), type of bill, sponsor, and status (e.g., 'House – at second reading'). By bringing these sources together, *LEGISinfo* offers easy access to legislative information and reduces time spent researching these matters.

Existing laws can be found on the Department of Justice's *Justice Laws Website* http://laws-lois.justice.gc.ca/eng/. All *Consolidated acts* and *Consolidated regulations* are available online, including frequently accessed statutes such as the Criminal Code, Income Tax Act, Copyright Act, Privacy Act, and Personal Information Protection and Electronic Documents Act. *Justice Laws Website* also includes Constitutional texts and the *Charter of rights and freedoms*. The Department's main website http://www.justice.gc.ca/eng/index.html details its judiciary and court systems, including court organization and roles, and links to various courts. In addition, *Canada.ca* contains links to acts, regulations, treaties with indigenous peoples, international agreements, bills before Parliament, the Canada Gazette, and laws and regulations relevant to any federal department or agency on its 'Treaties, laws and regulations' page https://www.canada.ca/en/government/system/laws.html

Canadian Provincial and Local Documents
The *publications.gc.ca* website contains links to the publications sections of the websites for each of Canada's provincial and territorial governments. Older provincial publications may be sourced from libraries in each state or province.
http://publications.gc.ca/site/eng/relatedSites/provincialTerritorialPublications.html

EXERCISE 11.5

Using the Canada.ca website (http://www.canada.ca) as your starting point, how would you find answers to the following questions? You do not have to answer the questions, just write down the steps you took to find the information. You may have to move from this website to other sites, e.g., for individual departments, or publications:

1. I need some basic information about the Chicken Farmers of Canada organization (it is associated with the Farm Products Council of Canada): what is it, when was it established, what is its role, has it produced any publications? Can you provide a link to a page within *Canada.ca* which will provide this information?

2. A mother has just heard about the possibility of an outbreak of Hepatitis A. Where can she find information on *Canada.ca* about it?

3. Where would you find information on how to start a small business in Ontario?

4. A recent widow needs information on the survivor benefits available to her through her husband's pension plan.

5. A college professor wants to know the status of Bill C-218 of the 42nd Parliament of Canada. The bill is entitled *An act to amend the Canada Transportation Act (railway noise and vibration control)*.

REVISION QUIZ 11.6
Use the following questions to consolidate your understanding of how to search for, and where to find, material produced by the Canadian government.

1. You have an Emergency Preparedness reference section in your public library. Search the catalog on the 'Government of Canada Publications' website at http://publications.gc.ca/site/eng/ourCatalogue.html for publications about earthquakes. Use the 'Advanced Search' option to search by subject. Select the titles that you think would be suitable for this section in your library. Indicate your initial search strategy, and ways you could refine it.

2. Answer the following questions for a patron, noting your search strategy and where you found the information:
"I understand the Government publishes an annual report of all the public opinion research undertaken by various government departments.
   a) How can I find this report?

   b) Which department commissioned research on the 2015 Christmas Lights display?

   c) What was the report number?

   d) Where/how can I view the results of the report?"

Australian Government Documents

In Australia, materials produced by government departments and government agencies are commonly referred to as *government publications*.

Like many other countries, Australia maintained a centralized publishing facility, the Australian Government Publishing Service (AGPS), that had responsibility for government publishing and printing from 1970 to 1997. In 1997 the production facilities of AGPS, including the Government Printing Office, were sold and the printing, publishing and distribution of documents became the responsibility of individual government departments and agencies. The growth of the Internet and the development of online publishing has resulted in most government publications now being available online.

The full publishing output of every government department is included on each department's individual website. In addition, the *Australia.gov.au* portal contains a section on government publications (http://www.australia.gov.au/about-government/publications) which is a good starting point for accessing recent annual reports, government gazettes, budget statements, parliamentary publications and Commonwealth legislation.

Each state and territory of Australia also maintains government websites that include publications from that state's departments and agencies.

Main Sources of Information about the Australian Government

For information about the Australian federal (i.e., Commonwealth) government, refer to:
- Federal government departments' Internet sites, that may be reached from the Australian Government portal at http://www.australia.gov.au/
- The *Australian Government Directory*, online at http://www.directory.gov.au
- The *Parliamentary Handbook*, available in print and from the Parliament's website (http://www.aph.gov.au)
- Ministerial press statements and press releases
- Government departments' catalogs of their own publications.

Types of Australian Government Publications

Australian government publications include legislation (acts, ordinances, statutes, bills and their explanatory memoranda, subordinate legislation and regulations), Budget Papers, Gazettes, government directories, Parliamentary Debates (Hansards), Parliamentary handbooks and Parliamentary papers, court reports, law reports, and annual reports, as well as subject-oriented publications by individual departments and agencies.

Annual Reports

Each Australian Commonwealth (i.e., federal) government department and agency is required by law to prepare an annual report to be tabled in Parliament. Annual reports inform Parliament and the public about the performance of departments and the services provided. They describe the role, functions, organizational structure, programs and key performance indicators of the department or agency for that year, and include statistics on staffing and finances. Annual reports are usually available as both print and electronic resources. All departmental annual reports are required to include an index, so the information within them is easily accessible.

Budget Papers

Budget Papers are published to accompany the annual Budget Speech of the Treasurer. They indicate proposed government income and expenditure for the coming financial year, as outlined in the Appropriation Bill, and contain important economic, financial and taxation information. More recent Budget Papers are often issued as a series of booklets covering financial topics, with the addition of budget-related papers on wider social policies promoted through the budget. Budget Papers are produced for the federal government as well as for each jurisdiction (i.e., State and Territory governments).

Gazettes

A gazette is an official publication for the purpose of notifying the actions and decisions of the government. All Australian governments (Commonwealth, State and Territory) publish official gazettes. Notices published in government gazettes cover all aspects of government concern and regulation, and most are published because of a requirement of law. Acts, regulations and other subordinate legislation are notified in all gazettes, with some states publishing regulations in full as part of the notification. Most Commonwealth and state gazettes now appear weekly, except the Special and Periodic gazettes which are published irregularly. Gazettes also deal with such matters as:
- proclamations that bring Acts into operation
- Public Service vacancies, appointments and promotions
- government tenders
- land notices: acquisition, disposal and transfers of property, leases granted
- lists of awards, honors, medals
- electoral notices
- government orders of various kinds
- private notices of a legal nature e.g., bankruptcies, company registrations and windings-up, probate, by-laws of companies under royal charter
- government purchasing matters
- local government matters
- registers of medical professionals.

Government Directories

Government directories are annual or periodic publications that provide up-to-date information on the institutions of government, their functions, their organizations, departments and addresses, and names of senior public servants. There are online versions of most of the current government state and federal directories, e.g., the *Australian Government Directory*.

Publications of Parliament

The Australian Parliament publishes the following:
- *Acts*—legislation that has passed all stages and been assented to
- subordinate legislation—statutory rules, regulations, by-laws
- *Hansard*—verbatim record of parliamentary debates
- *Votes and Proceedings* (House of Representatives) and *Journals* (Senate)—daily record of business

- *Notice Papers*—what business is proposed
- Parliamentary papers—papers that have been tabled, ordered to be printed and made available to the public. These include annual reports, reports of royal commissions and budget papers
- *Parliamentary handbook of the Commonwealth of Australia*—the official record of the Parliament, published for each three-year Parliament.

To obtain information about Parliamentary publications, use the *ParlInfo Search* page on the Parliament of Australia website at http://parlinfo.aph.gov.au/parlInfo/guide/guide.w3p, or the *Parliamentary Publications* section of the *Australia.gov.au* website at http://www.australia.gov.au/about-government/publications/parliamentary-publications.

Publications of the Judiciary
The Courts publish the following:
- official court records—*transcripts* of court proceedings, and *judgements* outlining key points of a case and the court's decision
- law reports—summaries of the facts of the case, concentrating on legal matters raised. Each state has its own series of law reports. Examples of federal law reports include:
    - *Commonwealth law reports* (decisions of the High Court of Australia)
    - *Federal Court reports* (decisions of the Federal Court of Australia)
    - *Administrative law decisions* (decisions of the Administrative Appeals Tribunal).

Other Departmental Publications
These include reports, newsletters, fact sheets, brochures, statistics and other information produced by departments and agencies in their subject area. The majority of these publications are online and can be accessed via the department's website. Many departments also produce online catalogs of their publications.

EXERCISE 11.7

*In what **type** of Australian government publication would you be likely to find the following information? You do not have to name the actual publication.*

1. Proposed government expenditure for the coming financial year

2. Lists of honors, awards and medals

3. Services provided by a government department

4. Specialist publications within a department's subject area

5. Addresses of government departments and agencies

6. Records of Parliamentary debates

7. Transcripts of court proceedings

8. Information about tax revenue

9. Financial reports of a government department

10. Summaries of legal cases

11. Information about the business proposed for Parliament

12. Job vacancies in the Public Service

13. Legislation that has been assented to

14. Proclamations that bring Acts of Parliament into operation

15. Names and positions of senior public servants

Selected Australian Government Document Tools
Statistical Information

The Australian Bureau of Statistics (ABS) is Australia's national statistical agency, collecting data and presenting statistics on a wide range of economic, social, population and environmental matters. The ABS website (http://www.abs.gov.au) not only provides current and past statistical data, it also maintains an 'article archive' of reports on Australian social trends from 1994 to 2014. Newer technologies like data sets, apps, and videos are also being used to present statistical information.

The ABS is changing its statistical infrastructure progressively from 2016 to 2021. It will be replacing many of its documents and products with new statistical data sets, and its website will reflect these changes. At present, the website is organized into two sections: statistics and census.

The Australian census is conducted by the ABS every five years, with the most recent in 2016. The 'census' section of the ABS website provides analytical articles, community profiles, data packs and data sets for the current census, and historical data for earlier censuses.

Handbooks, Manuals, and Yearbooks

The premier publication about the workings of the federal Parliament is the *Parliamentary Handbook of the Commonwealth of Australia*. It is maintained and published by the staff of the Parliamentary Library and is available in print or online at http://www.aph.gov.au/About_Parliament/Parliamentary_Departments/Parliamentary_Library/Parliamentary_Handbook. The *Handbook* includes biographies of all Members and Senators, details of the Ministry and Shadow Ministry, Parliamentary committees, statistical information on the composition of the Parliament, summaries of recent election results, the text of the Australian Constitution, results of referendums to change the Constitution, and historical information about Members and Senators since 1901.

The Australian Bureau of Statistics (ABS) published a consolidated yearbook, *Year book Australia*, from 1908 until 2012. This publication provided a statistical snapshot of the economic and social life of Australia as a whole, as well as statistical information about each state. The Bureau has now replaced the yearbook with online summary tables on various topics, available on the ABS website http://www.abs.gov.au. The website still provides access to all past yearbooks for historical comparisons and research.

Biographical Resources

The home page of the *Parliament of Australia* website (http://www.aph.gov.au) includes a link to 'Senators and Members', with photographs, contact details and biographies of members of the current parliament. This information is also available via the *Parliamentary Handbook*. The Handbook's online link to 'Senators and Members' brings you to the *Parliament of Australia* website and presents the same pages of information from that site.

Biographies of senators and clerks of the Senate serving between 1901 and 1983 are found in the *Biographical Dictionary of the Australian Senate*. This work is compiled by the Research Section of the Australian Senate and is online at http://biography.senate.gov.au or available as a 3-volume print publication. Biographies of senators and clerks who completed their service in the period from 1984 to 2002 are being prepared and will be added to the online web version, and possibly as an additional print volume, in future.

The *Parliament of Australia* website deals only with Commonwealth (i.e., federal) parliamentary members. Each state and territory parliament maintains a website, which has details of that legislature's members.

Although not a government publication, the *Australian Dictionary of Biography* is a comprehensive source of biographical information on deceased persons of note in Australian history (http://adb.anu.edu.au). The 'Advanced Search' option provides searching by occupations, including politicians and public servants. These occupations can be filtered by state or federal jurisdiction. The 'Faceted Browse' option allows repeated filtering to create a more specialized search among its categories of occupation.

Geographical Information
Geoscience Australia is the Australian Government's national mapping agency. It produces print and digital geographic, geologic, and thematic maps including the 1:1 million, 1:250,000, 1:100,000 and 1:50,000 topographic map series. You can access Geoscience Australia's map information at http://www.ga.gov.au/scientific-topics/national-location-information/topographic-maps-data. In addition, the *Australia.gov.au* portal contains a section on maps and mapping (http://www.australia.gov.au/information-and-services/business-and-industry/science-and-technology/maps-and-mapping). This is a good starting point for finding downloadable maps of Australia as well as maps for purchase.

All Australian states and territories provide online maps and geographic information for their jurisdiction. Each state or territory has its own set of available planning and land use information. The *Australia.gov.au* portal provides a link to these state services (http://www.australia.gov.au/information-and-services/business-and-industry/science-and-technology/online-mapping-services).

Geoscience Australia maintains the *National Gazetteer Place Name* online search tool (http://www.ga.gov.au/place-names), providing the location and spelling of all Australian towns, suburbs, roads and features such as hills, rivers, lakes and mines. Each state and territory also produces an online gazetteer of its place names. The Australian Hydrographic Service produces the *Maritime Gazetteer of Australia*, a searchable database containing all the place names used in Australia's official navigational charts for the mainland and offshore territories (http://www.hydro.gov.au/prodserv/publications/mga/mga.htm).

Bibliographies
Because Australian federal government publishing is the responsibility of individual government departments and agencies, there is no consolidated whole-of-government bibliography of government publications. Each federal government department and agency maintains a list of its publications on its website. Most state government websites have a publications page for access to a wide range of state-produced documents, although South Australia and Tasmania follow the federal model and each department or agency lists its publications on its website.

The National Library of Australia's *Recent Australian Government Publications (GovRAP)* (http://www.nla.gov.au/librariesaustralia/services/rap/govrap/) is a monthly list of all publications from federal and state departments and agencies that were published during the current or previous year, cataloged by libraries and added to the national bibliographic database. Records are arranged alphabetically by title and also in Dewey classified sequence. GovRAP lists, however, are only kept for the last six months.

Libraries that are members of the *Libraries Australia* network maintained by the National Library of Australia (http://www.nla.gov.au/librariesaustralia/) can search the Australian National Bibliographic Database by author, title or subject and limit results to 'Government'. Such searches will retrieve government publications from all jurisdictions, published at any time.

Directories
The *Australian Government Directory* (http://www/directory.gov.au) is the most comprehensive source of contact details for agencies and senior officials in the Australian government, and also provides descriptions of their functions. The directory provides details of federal departments and agencies, councils, committees and boards, and contact numbers by subject. There are links to the *Australian Government Organisations Register*, legislation administered by Australian government agencies, and specialist directories for the courts, Parliament and the Governor General (in the section titled 'Downloadable Reports'). The site also gives links to each of the state and territory directories.

The *Australia.gov.au* portal also provides a link to the Australian Government directory from its 'Contact Government' page http://www.australia.gov.au/about-government/contact-government. Much of the portal's information repeats what is found in the Directory, but the portal's link to 'State, territories and local government' http://www.australia.gov.au/about-government/states-territories-and-local-government provides additional details about the functions of government departments, as well as local government directories for each state.

Legislative and Judicial Information
The *Federal Register of Legislation* (http://www.legislation.gov.au) contains the full text of Commonwealth bills, laws and legislative instruments, as well as the Constitution and copies of the Commonwealth Government Gazette from 1901 to 2012. The *Australia.gov.au* portal 'Legislation' page http://www.australia.gov.au/information-and-services/public-safety-and-law/legislation provides links to Commonwealth, state and territory legislation as well as legal opinions, legal guides and frequently asked questions about legislation.

Although not a government agency, the *Australian Legal Information Institute (Austlii)*, a joint facility run by university faculties of law, is an authoritative source of legal information. The Austlii case and legislation database (http://www.austlii.edu.au/databases.html) provides a consolidated list of case law, legislation, rulings and determinations from all Australian jurisdictions.

Judicial information is available from the Commonwealth Attorney-General's Department website. It's 'Legal system' pages detail the judiciary and federal courts, with links to the state Supreme Courts https://www.ag.gov.au/LegalSystem/Pages/default.aspx. The *Australia.gov.au* portal 'Courts and tribunals' page http://www.australia.gov.au/information-

and-services/public-safety-and-law/courts-and-tribunals links to a range of courts and tribunals, and also links to state and territory information on Justices of the Peace.

Australian State, Territory and Local Government Documents

Each Australian state and territory maintains a website that can be accessed through the *Australia.gov.au* portal home page. These websites either contain a 'publications' page linking to all documents produced by their state departments, or links to individual state department websites that contain details of that department's publications.

Local government councils (also called *shire councils*) have websites accessible via links in their state or territory's government website. Documents not available electronically from the websites can often be located through local libraries. Local public libraries are the responsibility of shire councils in Australia, and many provide online catalogs on the council website.

ACTIVITY 11.8

*Use Australian government sources to find a variety of information about **one** of the following topics. Use a range of tools and resources, e.g., publications (reports, legislation, debates, statistics etc.), organizations (departments, committees etc.), people (proposer of bills, minister, head of department, committee member etc.). You can work at the federal or state level. Record the information found and the sources used to find it.*

- *Aboriginal & Torres Strait Islander welfare*
- *Child care*
- *Cost of living*
- *Dairy farming*
- *Free trade agreements*
- *Great Barrier Reef*
- *Housing*
- *Immigrants*
- *Juvenile detention*
- *Medical research*
- *Road transport*
- *Soldiers deployed in conflicts*
- *Tertiary education*
- *Trade unions*
- *Unemployment*

CHAPTER TWELVE
Specialized Information Sources

Introduction
Sometimes you will not be able to answer a reference inquiry using the tools mentioned so far, but will need other specialized sources of information. These sources include:
- international organizations
- non-governmental organizations
- statistical sources
- readers' advisory sources
- subject resources in the library's collection.

International Organization Sources
International organizations are broader in nature than individual governments and can provide a global perspective on issues. Many international organizations produce publications and data that can assist with reference queries. By far the most prolific, and often most useful, resources are those produced by the various bodies and agencies of the United Nations (UN).

United Nations Documents
The United Nations has six principal organs (or sections) and 15 special agencies. Publications are accessible at the UN's 360 depository libraries in over 134 countries, and many are also available online. The Dag Hammarskjöld Library (https://library.un.org/), located at UN headquarters in New York, provides links to its databases and other UN resources as a service to researchers and librarians (https://library.un.org/content/services-researchers-and-librarians). The Library is a good starting point for UN documents. Its website includes research guides to UN material (http://research.un.org) and a link to the Official Documents System (ODS) database.

The United Nations Official Document System (ODS) is an online database of UN documents that includes scanned documents published between 1946 and 1993, and full-text digital documents from 1993 onwards (https://documents.un.org/prod/ods.nsf/home.xsp). United Nations documents are available in the six official languages of the United Nations: Arabic, Chinese, English, French, Russian and Spanish. Some documents are also available in German. Documents are stored in text format or as PDF files.

Classification of UN Documents
UN documents are classified according to their producing bodies, such as General Assembly, Economic & Social Council, Security Council, Trusteeship Council, Secretariat, and various committees or programs. Further divisions indicate departments or series. The classification number is a combination of letters, numbers and slashes, beginning with a code for one of the principal organs or committees.

For example:

A/	General Assembly
E/	Economic & Social Council
S/	Security Council
T/	Trusteeship Council
ST/	Secretariat
CCPR/	Human Rights Committee
DP/	UN Development Program

This is followed by additional information on dates or session numbers, nature of document, and document type.

 For example:

A/52/100	General Assembly document from the fifty-second session
S/1997/100	Security Council document issued in 1997
E/1997/100	Economic and Social Council document from the 1997 sessions
ST/AI/405	Administrative instruction issued by the Secretariat

 Sara Striner's 'Guide to accessing United Nations publications at the Library of Congress', (https://www.loc.gov/rr/news/unguide.html) gives a more detailed explanation of the scheme. It was compiled in 1995, but is still relevant today.

United Nations Databases
In addition to the Official Documents System (ODS), the United Nations maintains a number of other databases that are outlined at http://www.un.org/en/databases/index.html. Those of particular relevance for general reference queries are:
- **UNBISnet** (United Nations Bibliographic Information System) http://ubisnet.un.org—the catalog of UN documents and publications indexed by the Dag Hammarskjöld Library and the Library of the UN Office at Geneva. The catalog provides some full-text resources and also references commercial publications and other non-UN sources held in the library's collection
- **UN-I-QUE** (UN Info Quest) http://www.imf.org—a ready-reference file created by the Dag Hammarskjöld Library designed to provide quick access to document symbols/sales numbers for UN materials (1946 onwards). It also provides answers to frequently asked questions. It does not give full bibliographic details and does not replace other UN databases.

Many of the UN agencies discussed below also maintain specialized databases on their websites.

United Nations Agencies
The 15 United Nations specialized agencies are autonomous organizations linked to the UN through special agreements. Each maintains its own website. Each agency includes publications on its website, and many also produce extensive statistical data.

- **Food and Agriculture Organization (FAO)** http://www.fao.org works to ensure food security, improve agricultural productivity, and better the conditions of rural populations. In addition to publications, it maintains a statistics website at http://www.fao.org/economic/ess/en/
- **International Civil Aviation Organization (ICAO)** http://www.icao.int sets international standards for civil aviation air transport safety and cooperation
- **International Fund for Agricultural Development (IFAD)** https://www.ifad.org finances projects for better food production and nutrition among the poor in developing countries. Its publications section https://www.ifad.org/pub/overview covers reports, fact sheets, knowledge notes, policies and research papers
- **International Labour Organization (ILO)** http://www.ilo.org formulates policies and programs to improve working conditions and employment opportunities, and defines international labor standards as guidelines for governments. Its website contains sections on publications, research, statistics and databases
- **International Maritime Organization (IMO)** http://www.imo.org aims to improve marine safety and international shipping procedures, and to prevent pollution from ships
- **International Monetary Fund (IMF)** http://www.imf.org facilitates international monetary cooperation and financial stability, and provides a permanent forum for consultation, advice, and assistance on financial issues
- **International Telecommunication Union (ITU)** https://www.itu.int allocates global radio and TV frequencies and satellite orbits, and develops technical standards for global networks. The ITU's *ICT-Eye* http://www.itu.int/net4/itu-d/icteye/ is a portal for key information and communication technologies (ICT) data and statistics on topics such as broadband, internet use, and mobile-cellular networks, while the *ICT Statistics* home page https://www.itu.int/en/ITU-D/Statistics/Pages/default.aspx contains a statistics database and a range of regional and global 'fast facts' and statistical reports about telecommunications
- **United Nations Educational, Scientific and Cultural Organization (UNESCO)** http://en.unesco.org/ promotes education for all, cultural development, protection of the world's natural and cultural heritage, press freedom, and communication. Its *UNESDOC database* contains full-text publications since 1945
- **UN Industrial Development Organization (UNIDO)** https://www.unido.org promotes the sustainable industrial advancement of developing countries through technical assistance and advisory services. It maintains the *UNIDO Statistics Data Portal* http://stat.unido.org/home and a range of free online publications on its open data platform https://open.unido.org/index.html#/publications/.
- **Universal Postal Union (UPU)** http://www.upu.int establishes international regulations for the organization of postal services. The UPU publishes the *Postal Statistics Yearbook* and its website includes a postal statistics database and a database of postcodes worldwide
- **World Bank group (WBG)** http://www.worldbank.org/ comprises five affiliated institutions that provide loans and technical assistance to developing countries in order to advance sustainable economic growth. The World Bank's data and publications are available through its Open Knowledge Repository http://www.worldbank.org/en/publication/reference

- **World Health Organization (WHO)** http://www.who.int coordinates programs aimed at solving health problems in areas such as immunization, health education, and the provision of essential drugs. Its Global Health Observatory http://www.who.int/gho is a gateway to health-related statistics
- **World Intellectual Property Organization (WIPO)** http://www.wipo.int promotes international protection of intellectual property (IP) and fosters cooperation on copyrights, trademarks, industrial designs, and patents. It maintains a range of IP databases, classifications, standards and publications, freely available from the Reference web page http://www.wipo.int/reference/en/
- **World Meteorological Organization (WMO)** http://www.wmo.int promotes scientific research on the atmosphere and on climate change, and facilitates the global exchange of meteorological data and information
- **World Tourism Organization (UNWTO)** http://www.unwto.org promotes responsible, sustainable and universally accessible tourism as a driver of economic growth and development, while minimizing its possible negative impacts. It maintains a range of tourism data http://www2.unwto.org/content/data including the largest online collection of tourism publications and statistics at http://www.e-unwto.org/.

EXERCISE 12.1

Indicate the UN website that would be most appropriate for each of the questions below, then answer the questions.

1. I need a copy of the latest *World economic outlook*.

2. Locate a story from the field about reducing rural poverty.

3. What is the healthy life expectancy for those born in Sierra Leone?

4. What is the mission statement for the *Commission for Climatology (CCl)*?

5. Where would you find publications on tourism development? Name two titles you found.

6. Where and when is the next *World Summit on the Information Society* Forum?

7. Looking at the *World Development Indicators*, what statistics are available on women in development in Colombia?

8. Where could I find publications on the utilization of natural resources for the benefit of present and future generations? Identify three publications available on the website.

9. I want to read the WIPO Copyright Treaty.

10. What research is being conducted on inequality, instability and employment?

Other International Organizations
Intergovernmental Organizations (IOs)
These are organizations, like the United Nations, whose members are primarily sovereign states working towards political or economic cooperation in a particular region or subject area. Intergovernmental organizations are useful sources of data for reference queries and research, particularly for statistics and reports in their area of interest. Some useful IOs are:
- **Organisation for Economic Co-operation and Development (OECD)** http://www.oecd.org is a major source of comparative statistical, economic and social data. It produces 250 publications and 40 statistical databases per year, including the *OECD Factbook* and *OECD Economic Surveys*. For statistical data, *OECD.Stat* http://stats.oecd.org includes detailed data and metadata in 18 topic areas, covering OECD countries and selected non-member economies. Many OECD publications are free online. Government libraries of OECD member countries can access additional publications by joining *OLIS* http://www.oecd.org/general/olis.htm, a free service open to all government officials
- **World Trade Organization (WTO)** http://www.wto.org the major entity overseeing international trade and dealing with the rules of trade between nations. It facilitates agreements on tariffs and sets procedures for settling disputes. It undertakes economic research and analysis and produces publications and statistics on all aspects of trade. The WTO produces the annual publications *World Trade Report* (research on global trade policy), *Word Trade Statistical Review* (compilation of global trade statistics), *World Tariff Profiles* (bound and applied tariffs), and *Trade Profiles* (key indicators on trade in goods and services for 195 economies)
- **ISO—International Organization for Standardization** http://www.iso.org develops and publishes standards to ensure products and services are safe, reliable and fit for purpose. Its membership of 163 national standards bodies contribute to the 2,100 international standards that cover almost every industry, from technology to food safety, agriculture and healthcare. Standards must be purchased, although the ISO's

Online Browsing Platform (OBP) https://www.iso.org/obp/ui/#home allows you to preview the content of selected standards before purchase
- **Development banks** provide financing for national development, and financial advice regarding development projects. The banks are usually formed by a group of countries consisting of donor and borrower nations. There are a number of development banks covering different areas of the world, e.g., Asian Development Bank, European Investment Bank, etc. The major development banks maintain websites where they publish their economic research. These often include basic statistics (land, population, national accounts, balance of payments, external debt, etc.); key economic, financial, social and environmental indicators; and development outlooks for the areas they cover
- **Regional/continental organizations** e.g., *Organization of American States, African Union, European Union, Council of Europe, Pacific Islands Forum, Asian Cooperation Dialogue* are established to foster cooperation and economic integration among the member entities within a geographic or geopolitical area. They are good sources of data and publications when requiring in-depth information about the region.

Non-governmental Organizations (NGOs)

Non-governmental organizations, or NGOs, are independent from states and international government organizations. NGOs undertake a wide array of activities. There are charitable NGOs that work to assist people in need, operational NGOs that achieve change directly through projects, and advocacy NGOs that promote particular causes (usually social or environmental causes). NGOs are usually non-profit, and are useful sources for detailed treatment of humanitarian or environmental issues. Major NGOs include:
- **CARE International** (http://www.care-international.org) works to defeat poverty, address discrimination and achieve social justice, particularly for women and girls
- **Greenpeace International** (http://www.greanpeace.org/international) is a global campaigning organization that acts to protect and conserve the environment
- **International Committee of the Red Cross** (http://www.icrc.org) gives protection and assistance to victims of armed conflict, and takes action in response to emergencies
- **Médecins Sans Frontières** (http://www.msf.org) or 'Doctors without Borders' provides medical aid to populations affected by natural or man-made disasters
- **Oxfam International** (http://www.oxfam.org) is a confederation of NGOs focused on helping communities lift themselves out of poverty, and addressing the injustices that cause poverty
- **Save the Children International** (http://www.savethechildren.net) focuses on protecting children in need through education, health care, and promotion of children's rights
- **World Wildlife Fund** (http://www.worldwildlife.org) produces detailed reports on wildlife, forests, oceans and climate as well as supporting conservation and environmental projects.

Some international NGOs maintain semi-autonomous branches in various countries. Other NGOs operate at a more local level, working only in a particular country or region, e.g., the *Australian Council of Social Services, CanadaHelps, American Civil Liberties Union*, etc.

CHAPTER TWELVE Specialized Information Sources

EXERCISE 12.2

*Choose **one** international organization and **one** non-governmental organization from the list above or from organizations you find on your own. Fill in details for each organization below.*

1. **International Organization**
   Name and website of organization

   Purpose or mission statement

   Does the website include publications? Provide the page URL and brief details of the types of publications included (e.g., annual reports, research reports, etc.)

   Does the website include statistical data? Provide the page URL and brief details of the types of statistics included.

   Does the website include databases of information? Are they freely available? Provide brief details and the URLs of the database sites.

   What question/s could be answered from the information provided by this organization?

   Did you find it easy to navigate this website? Was the information readily available and presented in a format that would support answering reference queries?

2. **Non-governmental Organization**
   Name and website of organization

   Purpose or mission statement

   Does the website include publications? Provide the page URL and brief details of the types of publications included (e.g., annual reports, research reports, etc.)

   Does the website include statistical data? Provide the page URL and brief details of the types of statistics included.

   Does the website include databases of information? Are they freely available? Provide brief details and the URLs of the database sites.

   What question/s could be answered from the information provided by this organization?

   Did you find it easy to navigate this website? Was the information readily available and presented in a format that would support answering reference queries?

Statistical Sources

Reference staff are often asked to assist patrons in finding statistics—in fact, statistical queries are one of the most frequent types of questions encountered by reference staff.

We have looked as some statistical sources in previous chapters: Chapter Nine introduced statistical yearbooks for information on a variety of topics covering many countries of the world, while Chapter Eleven disclosed the broad range statistics available from government sources. Many of the United Nations specialized agencies discussed in the current chapter produce regular and highly authoritative statistical series, as do international organizations like OECD. Other sources of statistics include annual reports of organizations, and appendices to research reports in particular subject areas.

Opinion polls are another useful source of statistical data. While many polls deal with people's stances on political issues, polling can canvass views on other topics, including employment, consumer confidence, television viewing, alcohol consumption, gambling, motor vehicle preferences, etc. Major pollsters include AC Nielsen Ratings, Gallup Poll, Roy Morgan Research, Survey USA, and YouGov. Note that the credibility of the polling organization, size of the population polled, methodology used and how the survey population was selected can affect both the accuracy and impartiality of the results.

 Results from opinion polls are often not as authoritative as surveys from government sources.

Readers' Advisory Sources

Helping users find recreational reading (known as *readers' advisory* or *RA* services) requires knowledge of the library's collection, especially the fiction collection, and an appreciation of the range of fiction genres available. These genres include the following, as well as overlaps or *genre blending*:
- adventure—hero overcoming obstacles and dangers in fulfilling a mission
- fantasy—generally includes magic
- gentle reads—'feel-good' books; no strong language, explicit sex or violence
- historical fiction—set in the past, before the author's lifetime and experience
- horror—produces fear in the reader; often monsters or supernatural elements
- literary fiction—award-winning, provocative, multilayered, serious issues
- mysteries—includes a puzzle with clues to the solution
- psychological suspense—chilling; disturbing; plays with the mind
- romance—love relationship between two characters with a happy ending. Sub-genres include contemporary, historical, racy, realistic and paranormal
- romantic suspense—romance with an element of danger
- science fiction—speculative fiction, usually set in the future
- suspense—fast-paced, building of tension and uneasiness
- thrillers—action-packed; focused on professions: espionage, medical, or legal
- westerns—set in western U.S. about the land and men who helped settle it
- women's lives and relationships—strong women; domestic and professional issues.

Adapted from Saricks, Joyce G. 2001. *Readers' advisory guide to genre fiction*. Chicago: American Library Association

 There are many different interpretations of what constitutes a fiction genre. Saricks' work is one example of possible groupings.

Books on animals, arts and entertainment, biography and memoir, discovery, food, gardening, history, home improvement, humor, travel, and true crime are also of interest to recreational readers. In addition to the variety of content for pleasure reading, libraries provide resources in alternative formats including DVDs, CDs, e-books and audio books. All these formats can be used in readers' advisory services.

The Library Collection
The primary information source for readers' advisory inquiries is the library's collection, since the aim of RA is to suggest resources that are immediately available for loan. Knowing what is in the collection, and more importantly *where it is* in the collection, is essential when delivering RA services. For non-fiction material, the library's classification scheme and the catalog's subject headings are good ways to locate groups of resources for review. Fictional genres can be harder to find, but the library's subject catalog can still be a useful resource in these cases. Both LCSH—the *Library of Congress Subject Headings* list, available as free pdf files at https://www.loc.gov/aba/publications/FreeLCSH/freelcsh.html—and the *Library of Congress Genre/Form Terms for Library and Archival Materials (LCGFT)*, also freely available at https://www.loc.gov/aba/publications/FreeLCGFT/GENRE.pdf, provide a good range of subject terms under their respective 'Fiction' headings.

 The LCGFT list contains extra genre terms, different in some cases from LCSH. If LCGFT terms are used, they are coded as MARC 655 #7, with the subfield code $2lcgft.

Some public libraries are beginning to group their fiction collections by genre (similar to bookshop arrangements), and there are schemes for organizing school library collections by both genre (Shenton 2006) and theme (Vernitski 2007, Jouin 2008). Such schemes can be extremely useful for RA services.

Currently, most fiction collections are simply shelved as a single sequence and organized alphabetically by author. Even this arrangement can assist the RA staff. Knowing other authors who work in a particular genre will help locate similar works for a patron.

Book Reviews
A readers' advisory service is most effective if the library maintains an active acquisition program for current recreational reading. Readers' Advisory staff can assist by suggesting new resources for purchase. Book reviews in local newspapers and magazines are a good source of information about popular reading and should be scanned regularly. Even if a library has a standing arrangement with a book supplier for all new popular fiction, it is worth reading reviews in order to become familiar with the basic plots of the new items. This will help the Readers' Advisor make more informed suggestions to patrons. Synopses in publisher/trade journals, as well as book reviews in library journals or specialist publications like the *New York Times'* collections of reviews (http://www.nytimes.com/section/books), are also invaluable sources of information that can be used by RA staff in their work.

Readers' Advisory Tools and Websites

There are a number of tools that can be used by RA staff to assist in readers' advisory inquiries. Some are print publications like the American Library Association's *Readers' Advisory Guides* or Nancy Pearl's range of guides to mainstream fiction. Others are pages on individual libraries' websites, or on state library websites, that offer links to RA websites.

The largest and most diverse group of RA tools are readers' advisory websites. Websites focusing on readers' advisory services cover either a broad general range of material or specialize in particular genres or age ranges. There are a large number of commercial sites as well as some social networking sites like *LibraryThing* (http://www.librarything.com), where contributors share their suggestions of favorite reads. The American Library Association provides booklists, a wiki, and a list of published tools on their *Reader's advisory* page (http://www.ala.org/tools/readers-advisory-0). The *Australian and New Zealand resources for readers' advisers* webpage developed by the commercial company LibrariesAlive! and available on their website (http://www.librariesalive.com.au/RA_sites.htm) is somewhat dated but provides a good list of resources focusing on the Australia/Pacific region.

Lists of RA tools can be searched on the Internet. A good starting point is Wikipedia's *Readers' advisory* entry (http://wikipedia.org/wiki/Reader'_advisory), that provides links not only to print publications and websites but also to blogs, wikis and chat sites.

In summary, suggesting a title similar to the user's favorite books comes with experience and broad reading habits. Readers' Advisory staff perform this task by:
- knowing their library's collection
- regularly scanning book reviews and reviews of other library resources
- consulting print and online publications about 'good reads'
- monitoring readers' advisory websites.

ACTIVITY 12.3

Choose one of Saricks' fiction genres described above and imagine you are providing a readers' advisory service for that genre in your local public library. Visit your public library and, based on its collection, answer the following questions. (note: the library does not have to have a readers' advisory service in place)

1. How easy is it to find this material in the collection? Does the catalog provide any assistance for discovering the library's holdings in this genre? If so, how? If not, what other strategies can help find the library's resources in the genre?

2. How extensive are the library's holdings in this genre? If a readers' advisory service was implemented, would the collection be able to sustain a reasonable number of requests for material in this genre?

3. How comprehensive are the library's holdings in this genre? Is there a good mix of current and older material? Are some/many/most of the 'classics' of this genre in the collection?

4. What format/s are the library's holdings in this genre? Are most of the resources print publications, or are there e-books, talking books, DVDs, etc?

5. Using one of the readers' advisory tools discussed (e.g., book reviews, websites, books or catalogs, etc.) suggest at least one current publication in this genre that the library does not hold and should acquire. Note the tool used. How would you describe this publication to a patron interested in the genre? Why would this publication be a good addition to the collection?

The Library Collection as a Specialized Information Source

Specialist subject information tools may be included in a reference collection if the library has the luxury of space for this additional information. However, in small collections or those with limited space for a separate reference area, 'reference works' are often only basic ready reference tools—all other resources are shelved in the general collection.

It is therefore important not to overlook the general collection as a useful source of reference information, particularly for more detailed, complex or extensive reference queries. The library catalog can help locate reports on various topics, and many of these include statistics and results of research in their appendices. Journal articles, accessed through the library's periodical subscriptions or indexing services, can include current maps, photographs, statistics and other data. Most non-fiction resources contain bibliographies that can lead to further information. Older versions of current ready reference tools, particularly encyclopedias and yearbooks, can provide useful comparative and historical information. In short, all the resources of the library are rich sources of information for reference work.

CHAPTER THIRTEEN
Delivering Information

Introduction
The previous chapters have described how to find answers to reference queries. The next important step is to present this information in a manner appropriate to the user.

Presenting Information
The method of preparing and presenting responses to reference queries will depend on the nature of the inquiry and the type of library.

School library users often require material found in encyclopedias, journals, or books, on the library's shelves or on appropriate Internet sites. Ideally the librarian and teacher work together to guide the students through the research process. The staff may also prepare reading lists or bibliographies for students and teachers.

Research library users usually have more specialized needs. Many research libraries enable users to access the library catalog and resources from their own desks. Librarians may create links or bookmarks for important Internet sites. They communicate with their clients electronically rather than expecting them to come into the library.

Special library users often ask library staff to search databases to locate information. They give staff precise instructions on the required information, and expect library staff to make judgments about the quality, reliability, and currency of any material they locate.

Delivering Information
Results of reference searches can be presented in different ways:
- Ready reference questions may be answered on the spot, or by short phone calls or emails
- Database search results can combine one or more of the following elements: citations, abstracts and full-text. While full-text articles are usually the preferred option, libraries should ensure their licensing agreements for databases and copyright restrictions for full-text articles allow the material to be passed on to clients. If not, providing a printout or email of the citations may be sufficient
- More complex questions may involve compiling a bibliography to be forwarded to the client.

Preparing a Bibliography

A bibliography lists the materials or resources found in answer to the reference query. Bibliographies are usually arranged alphabetically, primarily by author. There are a number of bibliographical styles that can be used, and some disciplines require specific styles. The more common styles used include the Harvard style (or Author–date system); MLA (Modern Language Association) system; APA (American Psychological Association) style; and *The Chicago manual of style*.

Whichever style you choose, it is important to maintain consistency. The following should be included in the citations:
- list references in alphabetical order by the first author's or editor's name, with surname first
- if the author is unknown, use the title instead, ignoring the initial words 'the', 'a' and 'an'
- italicize or underline the title of the resource
- if no place of publication is given, use [Place of publication not identified] and if no date, use [date of publication not identified]
- include playing time for films and DVDs.

 Different formats of material need different information included in the bibliography. Ensure the following details are provided for their relevant formats:

Electronic Sources
- author(s), editor(s), compiler(s) or the institution/organization responsible for the resource
- title and subtitle
- edition
- type of medium (e.g., online, CD-ROM)
- information supplier if appropriate
- full address (including path if applicable) to find the resource
- date of access.

Books (Monographs)
- author(s), editor(s), compiler(s) or the institution/organization responsible for the resource
- title and subtitle
- edition
- place and date of publication
- publisher
- series.

Journal (Serial) Articles
- author(s) of article
- title of article
- title of journal
- issue details
- page numbers.

Non-book Items
- author(s), editor(s), compiler(s) or the institution/organization responsible for the resource
- title and subtitle
- edition
- type of medium (e.g., map, DVD) and playing time if appropriate
- series
- publisher
- place and date of publication.

Most bibliographies simply provide citations for the relevant materials and resources. If more information is needed an annotated bibliography can be prepared, containing brief abstracts of the resource and in some cases notes about why it is relevant.

Citation Tools

Citation management tools are online resources that allow you to record bibliographic details as you collect and cite the sources you use in your bibliography. Some citation tools can be used without charge; others have a free 'basic' version with the option of a paid version with more features. Some citation tools have been set up as commercial software packages. They are often free to students and staff of a university or organization to use, but are otherwise a paid service. Many can be integrated into common word processing packages. Some of the most popular citation management tools used by libraries are *EndNote, RefWorks, Zotero, Calibre, and Mendeley.*

 In summary, the method used for compiling and delivering information, and the detail included, will be driven by the type of library and its policies on levels of assistance to users. Cost, time involved and legal restrictions may all be factors affecting delivery of information.

EXERCISE 13.1

A library user asks you to locate ten books about education in Mexico published in the last five years. You are to:

- *prepare a list of the books giving full citations including author, title, place, publisher and date of publication*
- *locate libraries in your state or province holding copies of these books*
- *provide details of how much each book costs and whether it is available in hard copy as well as paperback*
- *present the information in a clear, legible style*
- *describe your search strategy*
- *list the sources you used to find this information.*

EXERCISE 13.2

A library user wants you to locate ten periodical articles on the use of voting machines in elections. You are to:

- *write down the questions you would ask the user to determine exactly what information is required*
- *find ten articles on this topic*
- *include the relevant information to meet the user's requirements*
- *present the information in a clear, legible style*
- *describe your search strategy*
- *list the sources you used to find this information.*

EXERCISE 13.3

A library user needs recent statistics on the number of United States citizens who travel overseas. You are to:

- *write down the questions you would ask the user to determine exactly what information is required*
- *find statistics on this topic*
- *include the relevant information to meet the user's requirements*
- *present the information in a clear, legible style*
- *describe your search strategy*
- *list the sources you used to find this information.*

 **ACTIVITY 13.4**

Work with a fellow student or colleague to conduct a role-play. One will be the reference person and the other will be a user who requires an annotated list of references on a particular topic:

- *interview the user to establish their requirements*
- *prepare the information*
- *follow a recognized citation style of your choice*
- *present the information in a clear, legible style*

 **ACTIVITY 13.5**
Consider the following situations. Explain how your reference interview, search strategy and presentation of information would differ to suit each users' needs:

1. A child comes into a public library and asks for information on earthquakes.

2. An adult comes into a public library and asks for information on earthquakes.

3. An adult comes into a special geological library and asks for information on earthquakes.

CHAPTER FOURTEEN
Evaluating Reference Services

Introduction
Evaluating reference services can help staff determine the quality and value of the services they provide. Evaluation can be conducted in a range of ways, from staff performance appraisals to collecting statistics that can be used to understand the needs of users. The evaluation of reference services should consider:
- service inputs
- service outputs
- service outcomes.

Service Inputs
The service inputs in reference services refer to:
- reference resources
- the physical environment in the reference area
- staff.

Reference Resources
Assessing materials within a library's collection is an aspect of collection management closely related to reference services. A quality reference collection must contain useful and up-to-date resources. A helpful way to choose and evaluate appropriate resources for any reference collection is by checking standard lists of recommended materials.

Criteria for selecting reference materials include: currency; accuracy; authority; aim or purpose; scope; bias or slant; arrangement; bibliography; quality of index; format; need; and cost. Each of these factors is addressed in Chapter Five. De-selection, or *weeding*, involves many of the same elements. Reference titles should be updated on a regular schedule, depending on the library's budget and user needs. Maintaining current electronic and print reference tools is essential to keep the reference collection relevant.

Physical Environment
The building, space allocation, and arrangement of the reference area make a strong impression on user perceptions, regardless of the level of reference service provided. Therefore, to assist users, it is important to ensure that the reference area is well signposted and, if using a reference desk, to have it in a visible location.

Providing enough workstations, photocopy machines, email access and other equipment for patrons also relates to the reference service, as explained in Chapter Two.

Staff

Competencies for excellence of reference staff have been identified by the Reference and User Services Association, a division of the American Library Association in their guideline document *Professional competencies for reference and user services librarians* http://www.ala.org/rusa/resources/guidelines/professional. The competencies focus on the "abilities, skills, and knowledge that make the reference and user services librarians unique from other professionals". The document identifies goals and strategies:

- **access**—develop responsiveness to users; provide organization and design of services to meet the needs of the community; and employ critical thinking and analysis of information sources and services
- **knowledge base**—conduct environmental scanning to update developments in reference and user services; use new knowledge to enhance reference practices; share expertise with colleagues; contribute to improving professional practice through projects and independent learning
- **marketing/awareness/informing**—assess reference services; communicate reference services; and evaluate marketing efforts and information services
- **collaboration**—partner with user in seeking information; collaborate with colleagues to provide quality service; establish relations within the profession; maintain professional partnerships beyond the library
- **evaluation and assessment of resources and service**—survey users; assess information services; evaluate resources; determine technology needs; consider options in format, access, and presentation; and measure staff performance.

Scheduling the appropriate number of staff for the reference area is essential to maintain an effective reference service. This will require an examination of staffing patterns, including the levels and type of staff rostered at any given time. The impact of alternative staffing arrangements should be tested to judge the effects of queues at the desk, particularly in peak periods. When working in public areas staff should be easily identifiable, with a badge or some other distinguishing feature.

Service Outputs

Service outputs can be gauged by assessing reference transactions, including the advice, instruction, and assistance given; questions answered; and interactions between staff and clients. This may be done using:

- records of reference transactions made by staff—ideally using standard forms, either electronically or in print
- checklists (filled in by peers or self-evaluation by staff) to assess performance and reference skills
- unobtrusive observation—questions asked by 'mystery shoppers'.

Reference Transactions

Most reference sections keep statistics on their reference transactions to measure how busy they are, or to justify their staffing levels. However, the amount of information collected by different libraries varies immensely and there is no uniform way that queries are counted. Libraries may:

- distinguish between 'reference' questions and 'directional' questions
- differentiate 'quick reference' questions from 'research' questions
- count 'technical' questions about computers, printers, or the network separately while others include them under the banner of 'reference' questions, and some do not count technical questions at all
- have a category for 'referrals' to other subject specialists
- track the time of day and day of the week when questions are asked at the reference desk
- track the section or department and job title of the user
- collect reference desk data daily
- sample, for example, two randomly selected days per month, two weeks per year, or two weeks per quarter
- include questions that go directly to a reference staff member via telephone or personal email
- include chat reference questions
- track the length of reference transactions
- track the number of reference questions answered using electronic resources.

Forms

Often libraries have a printed form that sits at the reference desk to record the number of questions asked. Some use the form to record the details of a search such as the sources used, the time taken to answer the query and whether the search was successful. In an ideal situation, reference staff should record all details of an information search and maintain appropriate statistics of these inquiries. The types of forms and records vary with different types of libraries.

Electronic Reference Tracking

Increasingly, reference statistics are being maintained electronically through electronic reference tracking facilities rather than on paper. Information on electronic reference transactions can be collected and archived as part of ongoing library operations much more easily than information from traditional reference statistics.

Tracking reference queries provides an easy way to assess the questions that clients ask, and identifies any questions that are asked repeatedly. Reference staff can create a 'Frequently Asked Questions' page based on these questions or prepare pathways or library guides with appropriate information and bibliographic resources. This data can also become the basis of a knowledgebase, with documented answers that can provide rapid response to patrons.

The ease of collecting information about reference transactions does, however, raise issues concerning privacy. It is important to ensure information that could reveal a client's identity should be restricted.

Checklists

Checklists identify the key tasks to be completed by a staff member working within the reference service. Checklists are often created so that reference staff can assess their capabilities to complete on-the-job tasks. Alternatively, a checklist may assess a staff member's performance and their reference skills. The checklist may be filled in by a work colleague or it may involve self-evaluation by the staff member.

Unobtrusive Observation

Unobtrusive evaluation can be accomplished by sending 'mystery shoppers' to ask questions that can be measured for correct and complete answers. Traditionally, unobtrusive observation was used as a method of assessing reference answer accuracy, but it can also assess such things as staff interpersonal skills. Unobtrusive observation methods can be used effectively in a face-to-face or virtual environment. Reference questions can be prepared and answers determined for factual types of questions.

ACTIVITY 14.1

Visit a library and ask the reference staff if you can look at the methods they use to record:

- *the number of reference inquiries*
- *the types of reference inquiries*
- *the level of success answering reference inquiries*

Then answer the following questions.

1. What information is collected about reference inquiries?

2. What information is not collected about reference inquiries?

3. What other information could be collected?

4. What are the benefits of this method of data gathering?

5. Are there any problems with this method of data gathering?

6. How effective are the methods used in this library for gathering data about reference inquiries?

Service Outcomes

Ongoing evaluation is essential for the continued enhancement of reference services. Service outcomes show the benefit of reference services to users and the wider community, and can be gauged by the satisfaction of users and their views toward the services provided. Service outcomes can be measured using:
- user surveys and questionnaires
- interviews and focus groups
- observation
- case studies.

Deciding on the best method to use for evaluating reference services requires careful analysis of the strengths and weaknesses of each method. At times it may be appropriate to combine two or more methods to collect the most reliable and valid information.

User Surveys and Questionnaires

Surveys or questionnaires study the attitudes and opinions of people on specific topics. This is an efficient way to obtain information from a large and representative sample of users. Surveys:
- can focus on users' experiences with particular reference transactions
- provide insight into users' perceptions and concerns
- target both users and the wider community—are there groups not being served or not aware of the services available?
- can be available in-house; online; via email; via telephone; or by post
- should use clear and unambiguous questions.

Interviews and Focus Groups

Interviews are discussions between two or more people to draw out comments or statements. Focus groups are a form of group interview that emphasizes the interaction between participants. Interviews and focus groups are valuable for identifying the information-seeking patterns and behaviors of specific populations. They allow users the opportunity to share their experiences, perspectives, thoughts, and feelings. To be beneficial, interviewers and focus group facilitators must receive careful training.

Interviews and focus groups:
- can be structured—following a predetermined set of questions
- can be unstructured—allowing users to guide discussion
- can help interpret or supplement information gained through surveys and observation by providing more in-depth information
- allow greater insight into common concerns and issues that emerge from the interaction and debate between participants.

Observation

Observation is most useful in studying behavior, as information may be collected from people as they behave in real situations. Observational methods are used less frequently than surveys to evaluate reference services, because this method requires a greater investment of human resources. Safeguarding against observational bias also requires training.

Forms of observation that have been used to assess the quality of reference services include:
- direct observation of the reference interview (when users and staff know that someone is observing them)
- observers disguised as patrons asking preassigned questions (also known as unobtrusive observation)
- self-observation by keeping diaries or journals of activities
- recording interviews with audio or visual equipment
- reviewing data collected as part of daily library operations
- examining information on reference transactions collected for another purpose.

Case Studies

Case studies generally use several methods to study an organization in order to provide greater understanding and evaluation through the data that is collected.

Case studies may be used in an organization where there is an opportunity to devote specific time to this type of research. Staff must have the time to organize information about a situation and analyze it by seeking patterns and themes in the data, and comparing it with other cases. A case may involve individuals, services, or anything that evaluators choose to examine through in-depth analysis and comparison. Case studies are often used by consultants, who are brought in to an organization to evaluate an aspect of its work.

Effective case studies require several steps:
- defining the purpose of the evaluation
- obtaining agreement from reference staff
- providing evaluation goals and objectives
- defining the information that must be collected to determine whether the objectives are met
- collecting the data
- evaluating and analyzing the data
- preparing a report.

The advantages of the case study method are its applicability to real-life contemporary situations. Case studies are an important asset when it comes to establishing proof that what you are offering is valuable and of good quality. Case studies may also offer insights that cannot be achieved with other approaches.

Conclusion

Evaluating reference services can help staff determine the quality and value of the services they provide—reinforcing where current services should be maintained and providing the justification to add new services. Evaluation can assess both the human and physical resources within a library to more effectively and efficiently manage them.

ANSWERS

Some of the suggested answers are, by the nature of the questions, only a guide. Use these answers to stimulate your own thoughts if you have difficulty with an exercise.

Answers are not included where each response is likely to be different (e.g., personal response, individual examples).

EXERCISE 1.1
1. ready reference
2. ready reference or research depending on how much information the patron wants
3. readers' advisory
4. directional
5. ready reference
6. research
7. instructional (or reader education)
8. ready reference or research depending on how much information the patron wants
9. ready reference or research depending on how much information the patron wants. Make sure the patron is not in need of medical treatment
10. directional
11. ready reference
12. referral
13. ready reference
14. instructional (or reader education)
15. research

EXERCISE 2.2
1. Team staffing or Reference consultation model
2. Integrated service point concept
3. Virtual reference
4. No reference desk
5. Outreach model
6. Roving
7. Virtual reference
8. Traditional reference desk
9. Tiered reference service, Reference consultation model, Team staffing
10. Reverse tier service model

REVISION QUIZ 2.3
1. A small select group of frequently used resources at the reference desk is sometimes called the *ready reference* collection.
2. A readers' advisor is a library staff member who advises readers on their choice of books, and generally assists in the use of the resources of the library.
3. Current awareness services include: alert services, bibliographies or reading lists, bulletins and newsletters, displays, journal circulation, journal title and contents page, lists of Internet sites, media monitoring, new titles lists, RSS feeds, selective dissemination of information (SDI), social media.
4.

1. Virtual reference	D. Reference staff answer questions electronically
2. Outreach model	C. Reference staff visit users where they are in an office or department
3. Roving	A. Enables reference staff to talk with users who do not approach the reference desk
4. Team staffing	B. All staff in the reference section work together on the reference desk

5. Factors that might impact on the provision of a reference service include: type of library, library function or mission, technology available, collection size, collection scope, budget allocation, workloads, staff expertise, staff training, client needs, client numbers.

EXERCISE 3.2
Questions you could ask include:
1. Do you know the nationality of Felicity Adams? How recent do the articles have to be?
2. What do you know about Richard Lovelace? What nationality was he? Do you know when he lived? What is he known for?
3. Do you know what subject area this belongs to? How did you hear about this term?
4. What types of statistics do you want? Which other countries are you interested in? How up-to-date must the statistics be?
5. Are you interested in a particular type of mammal? Do you want an illustration of the whole skeleton or part of the skeleton? Do you want a color or black and white illustration?

EXERCISE 3.4

1. Your only requirement is to identify the relevant materials, if any, held by the library—and if they are insufficient, to identify any materials that may legitimately be requested on interlibrary loan, or from any other information agencies that the client could legitimately approach.
2. Your best response would be to point out the range of atlases held by your library, the qualities the library looks for in an atlas, and the recommendations contained in atlas buying guides and guides to reference works. Invite the client to look at the library's atlases and find the publications that best suits his or her needs. If you have had a lot of reference experience with atlases you can point out the strengths and weaknesses you have found in various atlases. If you are unsure about any of this, ask a more experienced staff member to run through some of the issues.
3. You should refer the client to the legal section of your library's collection and assist the client to identify relevant material.
4. You should inform the client about the copyright legislation that would or would not allow him or her to copy the three chapters. There should be a notice near the library's copiers outlining the fair dealing provisions of the copyright legislation.

EXERCISE 4.2

Some strategies are suggested below. There may be other appropriate strategies, as Web searching is not an exact science! You often need to experiment to come up with the best strategy.

1. "Belted Galloways" in the box for *this exact word or phrase*
2. "symptoms" in *all of the words* and "ebola virus" in *this exact word or phrase*
3. "Edwards syndrome" in *this exact word or phrase* and either ".gov" or ".edu" in *Domain*
4. "attention deficit disorder" in *this exact word or phrase*, and "parents support" in *with all the words*, and ".ca" in *Domain*

REVISION QUIZ 4.3

1. The *search strategy* is the process of finding answers to reference questions in the fastest and most efficient way. The term *search strategy* is also used to indicate the search statements formulated to answer an inquiry.
2. Any of the following could be considered as part of a good general approach to creating a search strategy:
    - Break down complex questions into more manageable parts. See if the question can be restated or organized differently to find a suitable answer.
    - Think broadly about the resources that might satisfy your patron's information need.
    - Start with a dictionary or encyclopedia (in either print or electronic form) to provide some background information if needed.
    - Review the reference tools that are available in the library to determine what would be most appropriate. Remember to consider books, journals, online databases, government reports, etc. Consider whether there are specific online resources that would relate to the topic.
    - Use keywords and subject headings that are appropriate for the reference tools. Use broader terms and synonyms to expand into further information and narrower terms for more precise searching.
    - Know how to use the available reference tools, including those online.
    - Don't rely on just one search engine. Conduct your search using a few search engines and compare the results.
    - When examining a reference tool, browse the table of contents and index for appropriate terms. If it contains a user guide, read through it for additional details on how to use the tool.
    - Consider the format or media that is most suitable for the user.
    - Involve others when necessary. Don't hesitate to search for experts in the field or refer to a local expert. Going to another staff member, making phone calls to potential experts, networking, or asking others may provide a richer and more complete answer for the user.
3. An effective search strategy involves the following components:
    - clarify the problem
    - prioritize sources and select materials
    - locate sources
    - search materials
    - evaluate the process
    - compile and present the findings
4. The following basic search features could be used when conducting searches:
    - capitalization
    - order
    - quotation marks
    - stop words

ANSWERS

5. Advanced search features that may assist in conducting a more focused search include:
   - Boolean operators: AND, OR, NOT
   - truncation
   - wildcards
   - phrase searching
   - proximity operators
   - nesting
   - searching specific fields
   - limiting
   - searching for information from a specific site

EXERCISE 5.4

#	Source	Clue
1	an atlas or gazetteer (an encyclopedia could also be used)	information about a place
2	an almanac	information about the calendar
3	an encyclopedia	information about a historical event
4	a dictionary of acronyms and abbreviations, or a dictionary of initialisms	information on initials or acronyms
5	a biographical dictionary	information about a person
6	a country yearbook or an encyclopedia	information associated with a country *Note:* you do not have a particular name to search so a biographical dictionary is less useful
7	a medical handbook	a concise source of information about a particular field of knowledge
8	a style manual	information on writing style
9	a children's encyclopedia	information relating to a child's interests
10	a periodical index or database	information about articles
11	a statistical yearbook	information on statistics
12	a bibliography or library catalog, or a literary encyclopedia	information about books
13	a business directory	information about companies
14	a government directory	information about government
15	an automotive repair manual	instructions on how to make something

190 LEARN REFERENCE WORK

EXERCISE 6.1

1. *Gramophone*—a British company
2. *The United Nations*—an international organization
3. *The New York Times*—a commercial company in the United States
4. *State Library of New South Wales*—a government organization in the state of New South Wales in Australia
5. *University of the Philippines*—an educational organization (university) in the Philippines

EXERCISE 6.2

#	Answer	Tool Used
2a	Goddess of wild animals, etc.	Use a resource listed under a heading such as 'Mythology', or 'Encyclopedias' or 'Factfinders'
2b	Federal Emergency Management Agency	Use a resource listed under a heading such as 'Acronyms'
2c	Saturday	Use a resource listed under a heading such as 'Calendars'
2d	40.7903° N, 73.9597° W	Use a gazetteer listed under a heading such as 'Gazetteers' or 'Maps'
2e	Any details about the Nicaraguan economy would be appropriate here	Use a general resource listed under a heading such as 'Geographical Resources', e.g., The CIA's *World factbook* or *Europa world year book*
3a	Eleanor Roosevelt was a U.S. First Lady	*Biography.com*
3b	Genghis Khan was born in Delüün Boldog in Mongolia	*Biography.com*
3c	Emma Thompson won BAFTA awards for two BBC TV series *Fortunes of War* and *Tutti Frutti*	*Biography.com*
4a	Sarah Flower Adams wrote *Nearer, my God, to Thee*	*Bartlett's quotations*
4b	Horatio Nelson said "England expects every man to do his duty"	*Bartlett's quotations*
4c	Douglas Jerrold said "A blessed companion is a book—a book that fitly chosen is a life-long friend"	*Bartlett's quotations*

EXERCISE 7.4

1. a general English dictionary
2. a dictionary of slang or colloquialisms
3. a dictionary of acronyms
4. a medical dictionary
5. a dictionary of usage
6. a dictionary of synonyms or a thesaurus
7. a dictionary based on historical principles
8. an Australian dictionary
9. a Spanish dictionary
10. a dictionary of quotations

EXERCISE 7.5

#	Answer	Tool Used
1	mind, psyche, mentality	a thesaurus such as *Roget's thesaurus of English words and phrases*
2	1562	a dictionary based on historical principles such as *Shorter Oxford English dictionary*
3	'How would you find him for a son-in-law?'	a dictionary based on historical principles such as *Shorter Oxford English dictionary*
4	imaginary means not real; imaginative means inventive, original	a dictionary of usage such as *Fowler's modern English usage*
5	an electrical instrument that sums up the value of the quantity measured with respect to time	a science dictionary such as *Chambers science and technology dictionary*
6	a sailor's short, heavy woollen overcoat	a general dictionary such as *Collins concise dictionary*, *Macquarie dictionary*, or *Random House dictionary*
7	a type of high-backed rocking chair	a general or American dictionary such as *Webster's third new international dictionary*
8	rire	a French-English dictionary such as *Cassell's French-English, English-French dictionary*
9	the technical name of a 'cold in the head'	a medical dictionary such as *Black's medical dictionary*
10	Lord Byron – described by Lady Caroline Lamb	a book of quotations such as *Oxford dictionary of quotations*

192 LEARN REFERENCE WORK

EXERCISE 7.9

Most of these questions could be answered by a comprehensive general encyclopedia; however, more specific types used to answer particular questions could include:

1. a general encyclopedia
2. a general encyclopedia suitable for children
3. an Australian encyclopedia
4. an American encyclopedia
5. a scientific encyclopedia
6. a general encyclopedia
7. a Canadian encyclopedia
8. an encyclopedia of the social sciences
9. a general encyclopedia
10. a foreign language encyclopedia written in Italian or a comprehensive English-language encyclopedia available in Italian translation

EXERCISE 7.10

Answers to each of these questions could also come from a general encyclopedia or a variety of other reference tools. The sources noted below are typical of those found in library reference collections.

1. an American encyclopedia such as *Encyclopedia Americana/Encyclopedia Americana Online*
2. a general purpose encyclopedia such as *World Book encyclopedia* will provide the answer: Sir Howard Florey and Ernst B. Chain
3. a specialist subject encyclopedia such as *Encyclopedia of psychology research*
4. an art encyclopedia such as *Grove encyclopedia of decorative arts*
5. a general purpose encyclopedia such as *World Book encyclopedia*
6. a specialist encyclopedia such as *Encyclopedia of library and information science*
7. a social sciences encyclopedia such as *International encyclopedia of the social and behavioral sciences*
8. a science encyclopedia such as *McGraw-Hill encyclopedia of science and technology*
9. a medical encyclopedia such as *The Merck manual/MSD manual*
10. a detailed encyclopedia such as *The encyclopaedia Britannica*

EXERCISE 8.2

1. an education directory
2. a newspaper or media directory
3. a directory of Australian associations
4. a directory of British universities
5. a directory of book publishers and publishing
6. a museums directory
7. a directory of directories, or a list of medical directories
8. a business directory
9. a Canadian or North American directory of associations
10. a New Zealand business directory

EXERCISE 8.3

#	Answer	Tool Used
1	Any disability journals from this directory would be accepted here	*Ulrich's periodical directory*
2	Dr Admasu Tsegaye (2016)	*World of learning*
3	Toyota Motor Corporation Japan, 1 Toyotacho, Toyota, Aichi, Japan	*Dun & Bradstreet 'Who owns whom', Far East volumes*
4	Yes	*Directory of Latin American universities and colleges*
5	Yes	*DOAJ Directory of open access journals*
6	Byblos Bank Europe, Rue Montoyer 10 - Bte 3 1000 Brussels, Belgium. Phone: +32 25 51 00 20 Website: http://www.byblosbank.com/Belgium	*Europages - The European business directory*
7	Any list of programs from this directory would be accepted here	*America's literacy directory*
8	Six: Rotorua District Choir; Te Wairere Library Learning Centre; National Forestry Library; Lakes District Health Board Library; Rotorua District Library; QE Health Library & Information Centre	*Directory of New Zealand libraries* http://natlib.govt.nz/directory-of-new-zealand-libraries
9	Mark Sims	*Guide to giving*. Probono Australia website http://www.probonoaustralia.com.au/directory#
10	Fresh Christmas greens and wreaths; Decorative plant materials; Decorative greens; Mosses; Fresh cut floral greens; Pine cones; Orchid growing media	*Innovation, Science and Economic Development Canada, 'Canadian Company Capabilities' page* http://www.ic.gc.ca/eic/site/ccc-rec.nsf/eng/home

EXERCISE 8.5

1. a biographical dictionary of filmmakers
2. a biographical dictionary for the medical profession
3. a general biographical dictionary
4. an international biographical dictionary
5. a biographical dictionary of musicians
6. a British biographical dictionary of the living such as *Who's who*
7. a biographical dictionary of the dead
8. a general biographical dictionary
9. a biographical dictionary of the dead
10. an American biographical dictionary of the living such as *Current biography*

EXERCISE 8.6

#	Answer	Tool Used
1	1492	*Chambers biographical dictionary*
2	1871-1874	*Oxford dictionary of national biography*
3	2007	*International who's who*
4	William Donald	*Who's who*
5	*Une Visite* (1955)	*International dictionary of films and filmmakers; Volume 2 Directors* **OR** *Biography in context*
6	University of British Colombia; Sir George Williams University, Montreal; University of Alta; York University; University of Toronto; University of Alabama; New York University; Macquarie University, Australia; Trinity University, San Antonio, Texas	*Canadian who's who*
7	Indio, Exton Elias, Avri Roel	*Who's who in America*
8	Nationality: Afghan Occupation: physician	*International who's who of authors and writers*
9	*The shepherd's crown* (2015)	*Who was who 2011-2015*
10	1996-1998	*Who's who in Australia*

ANSWERS 195

EXERCISE 8.8

#	Answer	Tool Used
1	*The master of nature photography.* Rosamund Kidman Cox, ed. New York, Firefly Books, 2013. 224 pages Penichon, Sylvie. *Twentieth-century color photographs.* Los Angeles, Calif., Getty Publications, 2013. 344 pages *Wildlife photographer of the year: 50 years.* Rosamund Kidman Cox, ed. New York, Firefly Books, 2014. 252 pages	*American reference books annual* – 2015 edition. volume 46. Santa Barbara, Calif., Libraries Unlimited, 2015
2	0749-176X	*The Standard periodical directory*
3	US$2800 for the first single volume, thick octavo, full contemporary mottled calf, gilt, black spine label. *Note: Honey & Wax Booksellers are selling this book*	*Bookman's price index*
4	Rising Star Publishers, Langley Park, MD	*The International directory of little magazines and small presses*
5	Kristin Hannah (published by St Martins Press, 2015)	*Global Books in Print*
6		*The Standard periodical directory*
7	Any of the awards from this directory would be accepted here	*Writers market: the most trusted guide to getting published*
8	Brunner/Routledge	*Information industry directory*
9	*The handbook of global science, technology, and innovation* (published by John Wiley & Sons)	*2015 Global books in print*
10	Any Toronto book retailer and antiquarian from this directory would be accepted here	*American Book Trade Directory*

EXERCISE 9.2

1. a statistical yearbook such as *Statistical abstract of the United States*
2. a yearbook such as *Europa world year book*
3. an almanac or yearbook such as *The world almanac and book of facts* or *Statesman's yearbook*
4. a manual—in this case, *Ford Focus owners manual*
5. an almanac such as *The world almanac and book of facts*
6. a handbook of mythology or an almanac
7. a guide to writing or style manual such as *Chicago manual of style*
8. an almanac such as *Time almanac*
9. a yearbook such as *World trade annual*
10. a yearbook such as *Statesman's yearbook*

EXERCISE 9.3

#	Answer	Tool Used
1	In a yearbook or almanac	*Europa world year book* **or** *The world almanac and book of facts*
2	In a yearbook	CIA's *World factbook* **or** *Far East and Australasia* **or** *Europa world year book*
3	Yes	*The Cambridge factfinder*
4	Wisma Nugra Santana, 9th Floor, Jalan Jenderal Sudirman 8, Jakarta	*Far East and Australasia* **or** *Europa world year book*
5	to show possession or to contract two words (although apostrophes are avoided in scientific reports)	a style manual such as *Chicago manual of style* **or** an almanac
6	In a book of records	*Guinness book of world records*
7	a number of minerals would be accepted here, gold and salt being two of the major ones produced	*The world almanac and book of facts* **or** *Europa world year book* **or** *Statesman's yearbook*
8	George Washington Gale Ferris Jr invented the Ferris Wheel, which was first erected for the 1983 Chicago World's Columbian Exposition	*The world almanac and book of facts* **or** *World almanac for kids*
9	In a library-based publication	*The Library and Book Trade Almanac*
10	In a compendium of facts	*The world almanac and book of facts*

ANSWERS 197

EXERCISE 10.2

1. an online digital map
2. a general atlas
3. a thematic map
4. a star map or celestial map
5. a historical atlas or historical map
6. a general atlas, or German national atlas
7. an interactive map produced by GIS
8. a relief map
9. a gazetteer or place names book
10. a travel guidebook

EXERCISE 10.3

The answers were found in a general atlas such as *Times comprehensive atlas of the world*

1. Parana, Brazil
2. Fairborn, USA
3. Storvik, Sweden
4. Strasbourg, France
5. Malaut, India
6. Engan, Norway
7. Benevento, Italy
8. Minyip, Australia
9. Mobara, Japan
10. Marys Harbour, Canada

EXERCISE 11.1

1. C—Commerce Department
2. NAS—National Aeronautical and Space Administration
3. NS—National Science Foundation
4. D—Defense Department
5. I—Interior Department
6. SI—Smithsonian Institution
7. A—Agriculture
8. ED—Education Department
9. Y—Congress
10. PREX—Executive Office of the President

EXERCISE 11.2

1. *Official congressional directory*
2. *Crime in the United States/Uniform crime reports*
3. *Catalog of U.S. government publications*
4. *AGRICOLA* database
5. U.S. census, or *Statistical abstract of the United States*
6. *Congress.gov* website
7. *Congressional pictorial directory*
8. *ERIC* database
9. *PubMed* or *MEDLINE* database
10. *World factbook* (CIA)

EXERCISE 11.4

1. Search the phrase 'farm debt mediat*' in Basic Search text box. (note, using * for truncation searches for mediate, mediating and mediation)
2. Search 'bees' in Basic Search text box, sort results by year (note, using 'bee*' returns too many irrelevant results)
3. Search 'air quality health index educat*' in Basic Search text box. This retrieves at least 4 items focused particularly on educational material (a search on simply 'air quality health index' retrieves items for all age groups). All are produced by Environment Canada. Those marked 'pdf' can be downloaded from the site, those marked 'paper' have bibliographic details provided so they can be obtained from the authoring Department or from a library.
4. Search 'lyme disease' in the Basic Search text box.

EXERCISE 11.5

1. On the *Canada.ca* home page (http://www.canada.ca), use the Search box to search 'Chicken Farmers of Canada'. Find the result from the Farm Products Council of Canada (http://www.fpcc-cpac.gc.ca/) page, which will provide all the information required. You could also choose one of the annual reports from the Publications Canada site (publications.gc.ca/collections …) listed on that page (although the information is scattered through the annual report), or instead of using the search option, choose 'Department and agencies' from the bottom banner of the *Canada.ca* home page, click on the Farm Products Council of Canada, and follow the links for agencies of the Council.

2. On the *Canada.ca* home page (http://www.canada.ca), use the drop-down 'Health' menu on the top banner and click on 'Health risks and safety'. Choose 'Public health notices' from the Topics page. This brings you to the Public Health Agency of Canada site, where the notices are arranged chronologically. You can scan the list, or search for the term 'hepatitis A'. For more information, search the Publications Canada catalog for documents about the disease.

3. On the *Canada.ca* home page (http://www.canada.ca), use the drop-down 'Business' menu on the top banner and click on 'Starting a business'. This will provide general information for businesses Canada-wide. For specific information about Ontario business, use the Government of Ontario's official website, *Ontario.ca*. Select 'Business + Economy' on the home page, which will take you to a page on starting and operating a business. There is also information on the 'Canada Business Ontario' website (http://www.cbo-eco.ca/en/index.cfm/starting/getting-started/starting-a-business/), which links to the material on *Ontario.ca*

4. On the *Canada.ca* home page (http://www.canada.ca), use the 'Most requested services and information' pane and click on 'Canada Pension Plan'. The resulting 'Overview' page has a link to 'Survivor benefits', which will provide the required information.

5. Use the LEGISinfo website (www.parl.gc.ca/legisinfo/). Choose "42nd Parliament, 1st Session" and scroll to C-218. Use the 'show details' button to see the status of this bill. If using the *Canada.ca* home page, it is best to search for the bill by its complete title. If you try searching by the bill number on the *Canada.ca* site, your search will have to include "42nd Parliament" "Bill C-218" as written here (i.e., in quotes), otherwise the results will return Bill C-218 of the current sitting of Parliament.

REVISION QUIZ 11.6

1. Begin your search with the simple term 'earthquakes' in the Subject field on the http://publications.gc.ca/site/eng/search/advancedSearch.html 'Advanced Search' page. Choose items from the results list that focus on the safety aspects of earthquakes, not the earth sciences aspects. To extend your search, check if your results bring up other terms you could try as subjects (e.g., 'emergency preparedness') or as text keywords in Basic Search (e.g., 'earthquakes AND survival', or 'earthquakes AND resistance'). You might also want to combine some of these terms with the names of any Departments or Agencies that produced relevant items, to see if there were other publications by them that could be useful.

2. a) Search the Government of Canada Publications Catalog 'Advanced Search' for the term 'public opinion'. Find the series entry for 'Public Opinion Research in the Government of Canada: annual report'. Check the results for the 2016 Annual Report, since the client wants information about research conducted on a 2015 project.
b) Table 1 in the 2016 report lists all the research projects. Scan the list for a likely title. You will find the Department of Canadian Heritage commissioned the research for the project '2015 Christmas Lights Across Canada'.
c) Report number POR 029-15 (taken from Table 1 of the 2016 Annual Report)
d) There is a link at the beginning of Table 1 in the 2016 Annual Report to the 'online collection of public opinion research reports' (www.porr-rrop.gc.ca) that are held in the Libraries and Archives Canada electronic collection. Use the 'Find a report' page to search this website to access the report.

EXERCISE 11.7

1. Budget papers
2. Gazettes
3. Annual reports
4. Departmental websites
5. Government directories
6. Hansard
7. Official court records
8. Budget papers
9. Annual reports
10. Law reports
11. Notice Papers
12. Gazettes
13. Acts of Parliament
14. Gazettes
15. Government directories, or Departmental websites

ANSWERS   201

EXERCISE 12.1

1. **Website:** International Monetary Fund
   Answer: use 'Publications' tab to find the latest copy in the series
2. **Website:** International Fund for Agricultural Development
   Answer: use 'Our stories' tab, 'Stories from the field' to find a story
3. **Website:** World Health Organization
   Answer: use 'Publications' tab, 'Key WHO publications' to find *World health statistics. Annex B Part 1*. The statistic in 2015 was 44.4
4. **Website:** World Meteorological Organization
   Answer: use link to 'Commission for Climatology' to find this Mission Statement: "To stimulate, lead, implement, assess and coordinate international technical activities within WMO under the World Climate Programme and the Global Framework for Climate Services to obtain and apply climate information and knowledge in support of sustainable socio-economic development and environmental protection"
5. **Website:** World Tourism Organization
   Answer: use link to 'Publications' at bottom of the home page, and choose two titles
6. **Website:** UN Educational, Scientific and Cultural Organization
   Answer: use 'Themes' tab, 'Building Knowledge Societies'; link to 'World Summit on the Information Society' to find the next Forum is 12-16 June 2017 in Geneva, Switzerland
7. **Website:** World Bank
   Answer: use 'Data' tab, link to *World Development Indicators*. Access the statistical tables to find that statistics about women include: Life expectancy at birth; Women who were first married by age 18; Account at a financial institution; Wage and salaried workers; Female part-time employment; Firms with female participation in ownership; Female legislators, senior officials, and managers; Women in parliaments; Nondiscrimination clause mentions gender in the constitution
8. **Website:** Food and Agriculture Organization
   Answer: use 'Publications' tab and choose three appropriate publications
9. **Website:** World Intellectual Property Organization
   Answer: use 'Policy' tab, 'Standing Committee on Copyright and Related Rights (SCCR)' and scroll to the link to the Treaty
10. **Website:** International Labour Organization
    Answer: use 'Research' tab, link to 'Inequality, instability and employment' to see current research

GLOSSARY

This glossary contains only those terms used in *Learn reference work*. For a more comprehensive glossary, see Farkas, Lynn, *LibrarySpeak: a glossary of terms in librarianship and information management*.

abridged A shortened or condensed version
abstract A summary of the essential points of an article or literary work; may be indicative, informative, or critical
abstracting service A bibliographic service that provides summaries of periodical articles, conference papers and chapters of edited books
academic library A library serving the information needs of the students and staff of a university or similar institution
access To obtain information from an information agency or database
acquisitions 1.The process of adding to a library's collection by purchase, gift or exchange. 2. The material so added
acronym A word formed from the initials of the name of an organization, system or service, pronounced as a word
alert services A tailor made service to keep users up-to-date with current news and newly published literature on a specific topic. Users are notified automatically when new content (e.g., online journal article, table of contents in a new issue of a journal) becomes available
almanac 1. An annual calendar with astronomical information and other data. 2. A miscellany of useful facts and statistical information
annotation A note of explanation or comment
annual (adj) Published once a year. (n) A serial published once a year
annual report An official publication reviewing the activities of an organization for a year
antonym The opposite of—eg 'good' is the antonym of 'bad'. Cf synonym
APA style A bibliographic format for citing information based on the requirements of the American Psychological Association. http://www.apastyle.org/
article A contribution to a serial written by one or more authors
atlas A volume of maps or charts with or without explanations
author 1. In AACR2, The person chiefly responsible for the intellectual or artistic content of a work. 2. Author: in RDA, a person, family or corporate body responsible for creating a work that is primarily textual in content, regardless of media type (e.g., printed, electronic or tactile text or spoken word) or of genre (e.g., poems, screenplays, blogs).
autobiography The story of a person's life written by him/herself
biannual Issued twice a year
bibliographic Related to books or other library materials
bibliographic citation A short description of an item. Elements for books include author, title, place of publication, publisher, and date; elements for periodical articles include author, article title, publication name, date, volume, issue, and pages
bibliographic database A computerized file of electronic records, each of which represents a bibliographic item that can be retrieved by author, title, subject heading, or keywords
bibliographic verification Confirming publication facts for an item including author, title, publisher, place of publication, dates, etc.

bibliography A list of materials or resources, usually either subject-related or on the works of one author

biennial Issued every two years

biographical dictionary A listing of people, usually in alphabetical order of surname, providing details of dates, titles, birthplace, family, etc.

biography 1. A written account of a person's life. 2. The branch of literature concerned with individual lives

bookmarking 1. Marking a place in a book. 2. Making a link to an Internet site so that you can return directly to it later

Boolean logic Use of the terms 'and', 'or', 'not' to formulate online search commands, to represent any logical possibility

Boolean operators A particular word used in formulating a search strategy to retrieve online information: **And**: retrieves only items with both terms; **Or**: retrieves items with either term; **Not**: retrieves items with one term and not the other

broader term A more general subject heading

browse 1. To examine a collection of library materials in an unsystematic way. 2. To look through a list of names, subjects etc., rather than going straight to a particular term

bulletin A publication of an organization (including libraries) containing information for members and/or users

call number A number on a library item consisting of a classification number, a book number, and often a location symbol

catalog A list of library materials contained in a collection, a library or a group of libraries, arranged according to some definite plan

censorship Prohibition against publishing or distributing material that is considered objectionable for social, political, religious or other reasons

chat reference Electronic reference communication in real time

Chicago style A format for preparing research papers and citing references, developed by the University of Chicago Press

circulation desk The area of the library where staff handle loans

citation Reference to a text or part of a text from which a passage is quoted, or to a source regarded as an authority for a statement or argument

classification A system for organizing information according to subject

collection development Planning the acquisition of material to build a library collection for the short to long term, to meet the needs of library users

concise Shortened, abbreviated

concordance An alphabetical index of the important words in a book, or the works of an author, with references to the phrases and passages in the text

conference proceedings The published papers given at a conference

confidentiality Respect for an individual's privacy; law in most countries, states and provinces protects confidentiality of library records

consortium A partnership or association of institutions, databases or services with a shared objective

contents page The page, usually at the front of a book or serial, that lists the contents in the order in which they appear

controlled vocabulary Terms found in an authoritative list of terms—e.g., Library of Congress Subject Headings, a database thesaurus

copyright The right given by law to authors, composers or publishers to sell, reproduce or publish a work during a stated period of time
cross reference Direction from one term or entry to another
currency Up-to-dateness
current awareness service A service provided by a library to keep users up-to-date with information in their interest areas
database A collection of records, usually in machine-readable format, each record being the required information about one resource
depository library 1. A library that is entitled by copyright law to receive publications on legal deposit. 2. A library legally designated to receive government publications free of charge
derivation Tracing a word to its source or root
dictionary An alphabetically arranged publication containing information about words, meanings, derivations, spelling, pronunciation, syllabication and usage
digest An abridgment of a written work, usually prepared by a person other than the author of the original
digital library A library in which many of the resources are in digital (machine-readable) format
directional inquiry An inquiry about where something is located
directory 1. A list of names of residents, organizations or companies in an area, providing various details—e.g., addresses. 2. A list of members of a particular profession or trade
domain name The address that identifies a site on the Internet—e.g., www.wcsu.edu, www.louvre.fr, www.abc.net.au
download To transfer a file from another computer to one's own computer
e-book electronic book. A book published in electronic format and made available via the Internet or for use on a portable electronic device
edition All the copies of a work produced from the same original
editor Person who prepares another person's work for publication
e-journal electronic journal. A periodical published in electronic format, and made available via the Internet
electronic resource e-resource. Any source of information available electronically, usually on the Internet
encyclopedia 1. A systematic summary of all significant knowledge. 2. A summary of the knowledge of one subject. Usually arranged alphabetically
eponym A word based on a person's name, e.g., Braille, Wellington boot
ethics Rules of behavior or conduct
etymology The derivation of a word, its origin and history
fair dealing Making a copy, for the purpose of research or study, of one or more articles on the same subject matter in a periodical publication or, in the case of any other work, of a reasonable portion of a work—i.e., 10% of the total number of pages, or one chapter
file 1. Systematically arranged records. 2. The container in which records are arranged. 3. A document created on a computer
form 1. The way in which bibliographic text is arranged—e.g., dictionary. 2. Type of literary work—e.g., poetry, drama

format (n) 1. Appearance of a publication—its size, paper, type, binding etc. 2. Layout or presentation of items in machine-readable form. 3. Physical type of an audiovisual resource—e.g., slide, filmstrip etc.

frequency Interval between issues of a serial—e.g., weekly, quarterly

full text Complete document

gazetteer A geographical directory listing places, their locations and information about them

genre A category of literature—e.g., novel, fantasy, science fiction, poetry

glossary An alphabetical list of definitions

Google A service that locates information on the World Wide Web - http://www.google.com

government publication A document prepared for or by a government agency, that is published and distributed for public information

handbook A concise ready reference source of information for a particular field of knowledge

Hansard The official report of proceedings in parliaments

Harvard style A format for citing references using author and date, developed by Harvard University

hit 1. The location of a relevant item in a computer database. 2. A match in a search for a bibliographic record

holdings Stock of a library or information centre

home page 1. first page of a website, that may serving as a table of contents for the site. 2. a web page set as the default or start-up page on a browser.

hypertext Information connected via links in the text, with a computer automating movement from one piece of information to another

index 1. An alphabetical list of terms or topics in a work, usually found at the back. 2. A systematically arranged list that indicates the contents of a document or group of documents

information agency An organization that provides access to information—e.g., a library, an archive

information desk The area of a library where staff help people to use the library and answer requests for information

information literacy The ability to recognize a need for information, and then to find, organize and use information

interlibrary loan A loan made by one library to another for the use of an individual, including the provision of a photocopy of the original work requested

International Standard Book Number ISBN. A number intended to be unique, assigned by an agency in each country to all books and pamphlets, book readings on cassette, microfiche publications, computer software and multimedia kits containing printed material. Identifies the publisher, language and title. Adopted internationally in 1969

International Standard Serial Number ISSN. An internationally recognized number assigned to each serial publication by the International Serials Data System (ISDS), a network of national centres sponsored by UNESCO - http://www.issn.org/

introduction A preliminary section that introduces a work

ISBN *See* International Standard Book Number

ISSN *See* International Standard Serial Number

jargon 1. The terminology of a profession or group. 2. Slang

journal 1. A periodical issued by an institution, corporation or learned society containing current information and reports of activities or works in a particular field. 2. A record of events, experiences, thoughts, and observations kept regularly by an individual for personal use

jurisdiction The authority granted to a legal body to administer justice within a defined area of responsibility. Jurisdiction may be applied at local, state, and federal levels

keyword A significant term in a document, that identifies subject content

language dictionary A dictionary with words in one language and definitions in the other; may be in two parts with words in the second language and definitions in the first as well

legal deposit The law that obliges publishers to deposit copies of their publications in libraries in the country in which they are published, including the national library and other libraries designated in the Act

letter-by-letter alphabetizing Arranging in strict alphabetical order ignoring word breaks—e.g., Newbery before New England.

lexicon A dictionary, most often of ancient languages

librarian A person with a library qualification recognized as professional by the relevant library association, or performing work at a professional level

librarianship 1. The profession of the people who staff libraries, and the management of libraries and library services. 2. The professional knowledge and skill with which recorded information is selected, acquired, organized, stored, maintained, retrieved, and disseminated to meet the needs of clients

library 1. A collection of books and other materials for reading, study or reference. 2. A place housing a collection of materials for reading, study or reference, or from which to borrow

Library of Congress Subject Headings (LCSH). The authoritative list of subject headings compiled and maintained by the Library of Congress. Available in print until 2014 and online as part of the Library's Classification Web - http://www.loc.gov/aba/cataloging/subject/

library guide A guide to the resources of a particular subject area, developed by library staff and usually held by their library

library technician 1. A person with a qualification in librarianship recognized as paraprofessional by the relevant library association, or performing work at a paraprofessional level. 2. (PNG) Designation introduced in 1982 to encompass the duties of library assistant and library officer

link 1. A keyword, phrase or graphic on the Web that connects to another web page. 2. A connection between two files or data items so that a change in one is reflected by a change in the second

literature search A systematic and thorough search for information on a topic

loan A recorded transaction in which a borrower removes an item from a collection for a stated period of time

location symbol A symbol showing the collection in which an item belongs—e.g., F for fiction

manual (adj) Without the use of a computer. (n) A book of instruction on doing, making or performing something

map A representation, normally to scale, of an area of the earth's surface or another celestial body

MARC MAchine-**R**eadable Cataloging. A format developed by the Library of Congress in 1966 so that libraries can share machine-readable bibliographic data. The MARC data elements are the foundation of many library catalogs

media monitoring A service that examines the press, radio and television regularly for information on specific topics, and reports to requesting clients

menu-driven program A computer program that provides menus for choosing options

microfiche A microfilmed transparency about the size and shape of a filing card, that may have on it many pages of print

MLA style A bibliographic format for citing information based on the requirements of the Modern Language Association - http://www.mla.org/style

monograph A publication either complete in one part or in a finite number of separate parts

narrower term A more specific subject heading

national library A library maintained by government funds and serving the nation as whole. It is usually the country's legal deposit library, and collects and preserves the nation's literature

network 1. A group of computers connected together to transmit information to each other. 2. Two or more libraries that share resources or exchange information

news summary A weekly or monthly looseleaf digest of news events, designed for storage in binders in chronological order

notation The series of symbols that stand for the classes, subclasses, divisions and subdivisions of classes in a classification scheme

obituary Notice of a person's death often including a biographical sketch; included in biographical tools such as *Biography index*

online Having direct access to information stored in a computer, having interactive communication with a computer

orientation In libraries, an introduction to the facility, services, and resources, to help people derive benefit from using the library

paraphrase To express the same thing in other words

paraprofessional A person trained to assist librarians and able to perform tasks requiring significant knowledge in librarianship, but without a professional (i.e., degree) qualification. Can include library assistants, library officers, library technicians

parliamentary paper A document presented to a parliament and ordered by Parliament to be printed. Parliamentary papers include annual reports of government departments and agencies, and reports commissioned by the government for discussion in Parliament

pathfinder Directions to the resources available for a literature search

patron A person who makes use of a service—e.g., a library patron uses the library

peer-reviewed Evaluated by at least one specialist reader, as well as the editor of a scholarly journal, before it is accepted

periodical A serial with a distinctive title intended to appear in successive parts at stated and regular intervals. Often used as a synonym for serial

periodical index A subject index to a group of periodicals, usually in a general subject area

phonetic According to the sounds of spoken language

precision A measure of the accuracy of database searching

preface The author's or editor's reasons for the book. It appears after the title page and before the introduction

primary source A document that provides first-hand knowledge of an event, including personal papers, photographs, etc.

proactive reference service Reference service where staff initiate contact with users

professional Having a university or equivalent qualification in librarianship or information management, and working at a professional level

profile An outline of the interest area(s) of a user or a group of users, used by the library to identify new information of interest to particular users. 2. An indication to a library supplier of the subject areas in which materials should/should not be supplied

projection A particular way of representing the earth (three-dimensional) on a map (two-dimensional)

protocol 1. A set of guidelines, regulations and requirements agreed to by all parties, often international agreements—e.g. the ISO interlibrary loan protocol. 2. An agreed set of rules by which messages passed from one computer system to another are encoded and interpreted

proximity operator A word or symbol that enables searching of terms close to each other in a title etc.—e.g., near, with

publication The issuing of copies of a book or other item to the public

public library A library funded by government that provides library services to all sections of the community

publisher A person or body that issues copies of a book or other item to the public

quotation book Reference book containing famous words; may be indexed chronologically or alphabetically by subject, author, or first line

reactive reference service An approach to service whereby librarians communicate with users only when approached or asked for help

readers' advisor A library staff member who advises readers on their choice of books and generally assists in the use of the resources of the library

reading list A list of materials or resources, usually either subject-related or on the works of one author

ready reference query A question requiring factual information from one simple source

real time online reference service A reference service in which librarians respond to online user queries immediately

recall (n) 1. A request for the return from loan of a library item. 2. Retrieval of information from a database. (v) To request the return of a library loan

reference collection A collection of resources intended to be consulted for factual information on specific matters, rather than read

reference desk The area of the library where staff help people to use the library and answer requests for information

reference interview The face-to-face, telephone or electronic exchange between a reference staff member and a user to communicate, refine or clarify a reference inquiry

reference services Services to library users including reader education, meeting users' requests for specific information and assistance, and managing the use of library material and equipment

reference strategy The process of finding answers to reference queries in the fastest, most efficient way

reference work 1. A resource intended to be consulted for factual information on specific matters, rather than read. 2. The work of the library that provides assistance to users seeking information

related term A subject heading at the same level of specificity to another heading and related in subject matter

remote access Access by users from outside the library; often requires authorization by name, number and/or password

resource sharing The sharing of material between libraries, such as where an expensive item is purchased by one library and made available to others

role play 1. Performing an imaginary role, especially as a method of instruction or training. 2. Acting out real-life situations

roving An approach to reference services that advocates moving reference activities to the floor of the library, rather than passively waiting behind a reference desk for users to approach with queries

RSS, RSS feed A 'push' technology in which online publishers send changes of frequently updated website content directly to users, eliminating the need for the user to check the website regularly

school library A library in a school that offers a library service to students and staff

scope note A note describing the range and meaning of a subject term or classification number

SDI Selective dissemination of information. *See* current awareness service

search engine Software that locates information in a database or set of databases, especially on the Internet

search strategy 1. The approach adopted to finding information on a particular topic. 2. The search statements used to answer a query

search term A word, phrase or number entered by a user to find the records in a database that match the term

secondary source A work that reports or interprets an event using first-hand documents

selective dissemination of information *See* current awareness service

serial A resource issued in successive parts, usually bearing numbering, that has no predetermined conclusion. One of RDA's four modes of issuance. Includes reproductions of serials, and also resources that exhibit characteristics of serials but whose duration is limited—e.g., newsletters of events

special library A library focusing on a specialized subject area. Usually maintained by a corporation, association or government agency

standard A published document that sets out the minimum requirements needed to ensure that a product, material or procedure will do the job it is intended to do

statistics Numerical facts often presented in a table

style manual A set of rules designed to ensure consistency of spelling, abbreviations, citation style etc.

subject heading A heading that describes a subject and provides subject access to a catalog

SuDocs number The call number of a U.S. government publication, assigned according to a special classification system maintained by the U.S. Superintendent of Documents—e.g., SBA 1.1/2-2 (Small Business Economic Indicators)

synonym A word with the same meaning as another

text The body or main part of a book

thesaurus (Plural thesauri) 1. A work containing synonymous and related words and phrases. 2. A list of controlled terms used in a database

tiered service Degrees or levels of service

title 1. A word or phrase that names a resource. 2. The entire resource, as in 'a number of titles'

title page The page in a printed resource that provides the most complete information about the author and title, and is used as a primary source of cataloging data

topical 1. Relating to matters of interest of the day. 2. Relating to a subject

trade bibliography A listing of books available for sale in a country, together with details of publishers etc. needed for purchase

truncation Abbreviation of a search term using a special symbol, such as * or ? , in order to include variants of the term such as plurals, adjectives etc.

unabridged Not shortened

URL Uniform Resource Locator. The address of a site on the World Wide Web

user A person who uses the services of a library

vanity publication A publication produced entirely at the author's risk and expense; self-published

vendor A company that provides serials, supplies, library systems, databases, and other products and services for a fee

verso The left-hand page of an open book; the back of a leaf of a book—e.g., verso of the title page

virtual library A library whose primary resources are electronic, and that provides access for its users to databases, images etc., including via other information providers

virtual reference Reference assistance by library professionals, given online to library clients who may email, post questions, submit reference forms or engage in interactive chats or instant messaging

web directory A web search tool in which websites are collected and evaluated by human beings, and organized under appropriate subject headings or categories, e.g., Yahoo!, Academic Info, Infomine

wildcard A symbol that replaces one character in a search term—e.g., organi#ation

word-by-word alphabetizing Arranging in strict alphabetical order within each word—e.g., New Town before newness

yearbook An annual publication containing current information in brief, descriptive and/or statistical form

BIBLIOGRAPHY

American Library Association. Reference and User Services Association. RSS Management of Reference Committee. (2013). *Guidelines for behavioral performance of reference and information service providers*. Revised edition.
http://www.ala.org/rusa/resources/guidelines/guidelinesbehavioral

Cassell, K. A. & Hiremath, U. (2011). *Reference and information services in the 21st century : an introduction*. 2nd revised edition. New York : Neal-Schuman.

Duckett, B., Walker, P. & Donnelly, C. (2008). *Know it all, find it fast: an A-Z source guide for the enquiry desk*. 3rd edition. London : Facet.

Ellis, L. A. (Ed.) (2016). *Teaching reference today : new directions, novel approaches*. Maryland : Rowman & Littlefield.

Farkas, L. (2015). *LibrarySpeak: a glossary of terms in librarianship and information management*. International edition. Friendswood, Texas : TotalRecall Publications.

Havard, L. (2007) How to conduct an effective and valid literature search. *Nursing Times*. 103 (45), 32-33. http://www.nursingtimes.net/nursing-practice/clinical-zones/educators/how-to-conduct-an-effective-and-valid-literature-search/217252.article

Jacoby, J., Ward, D., Avery, S. & Marcyk, E. (2016). The value of chat reference services: a pilot study. *Libraries and the Academy*, 16(1), 109-129

Jouin, S. (2008). "We need to talk about problem novels". A new way of classifying novels for a young adult readership. *Bulletin des Bibliotheques de France*. (6), 76-80

Katz, W. A. (2002). *Introduction to reference work*. 2 vols. Eighth edition. New York : McGraw-Hill.

Lane, N. D., Chisholm M. & Mateer, C. (2000). *Techniques for student research: a comprehensive guide to using the library*. New York : Neal-Schuman.

Miles, D. B. (2013). Shall we get rid of the reference desk? *Reference & User Services Quarterly*. 52(4), 320-333.

Mulac, C. M. (2012). *Fundamentals of reference*. Chicago : American Library Association.

Murphy, S. A. (2011). *The Librarian as information consultant: transforming reference for the Information Age*. Chicago : American Library Association.

Ross, C. S., & Dewdney, P. (2013). *Communicating professionally: a how-to-do-it manual for librarians*. Third edition. New York : Neal-Schuman.

Ross, C. S., Nilsen, K. & Radford, M. L. (2009). *Conducting the reference interview : a how-to-do-it manual for librarians*. Second edition. New York : Neal-Schuman.

Rowe, H. (2015). *Learn about information*. International edition. Friendswood, Texas : TotalRecall Publications.

Rowe, H. & Grover, T. (2015). *Learn basic library skills*. International edition. Friendswood, Texas : TotalRecall Publications.

Saricks, J. G. (2005). *Readers' advisory service in the public library.* 3rd edition. Chicago : American Library Association.

Shenton, Andrew K. (2006). The role of 'reactive classification' in relation to fiction collections in school libraries. *New Review of Children's Literature and Librarianship.* 12(2), 127-146.

Singer, C. A. (2012). *Fundamentals of managing reference collections.* London : Facet.

Smith, L. C. & Wong, M. A. (Ed.) (2016). *Reference and information services : an introduction.* 5th edition. Santa Barbara, California : Libraries Unlimited.

Vernitski, A. (2007). Developing an intertextuality-oriented fiction classification. *Journal of Librarianship and Information Science.* 39(1), 41-52.

Yang, S. Q. and Dalal, H. A. (2015). Delivering virtual reference services on the web: an investigation into the current practice by academic libraries. *The Journal of Academic Librarianship.* 41(1), 68-86.

INDEX

abstracts, 67, 169, 171
almanacs, 49, 56
annual reports, 148-149, 150, 165
Ask a Librarian, 15, 24
atlases, 49, 56, 114, 122
Australian government documents, 148-155
bibliographic databases *see* Databases
bibliographies, 12, 49, 136, 144, 153-154, 171
    preparation of, 170-171
Biographical dictionaries *see* Biographical directories
biographical directories, 49, 56, 98-100, 136, 144, 152-153
Boolean operators, 36, 38
Canadian government documents, 140-145
census data, 135, 143, 152
choosing
    biographical directories, 100
    databases, 68
    dictionaries, 76
    encyclopedias, 85
    organizational directories, 92
    reference tools, 5, 44-47, 56
citation management tools, 171
classification systems, 131-134, 135, 140-141, 157-158
collection development, 10, 177
communication, 21, 22-23
copyright, 29, 66, 134, 140, 145, 160
current awareness, 12
databases, 35-37, 66-69, 101, 137, 154, 158, 161
    see also Periodical indexes
    see also Index and abstract services
delivering information, 169
demanding patrons, 6-8
dictionaries, 49, 56, 71-76
directories, 91-112, 136, 144-145, 149, 154
directories, biographical *see* Biographical directories
directories, organizational *see* Organizational directories
directories, trade *see* Trade directories
domain names, 37, 60
electronic encyclopedias, 83
electronic resources, 46, 47, 66, 108

bibliographic citation, 170
licensing agreements, 66, 140, 169
    see also Online resources
encyclopedias, 49, 56, 81-85
ethics, 5, 29
evaluating
    dictionaries, 76
    electronic resources, 46-47
    geographic tools, 123
    Internet information 61-62
    library collections, 10
    reference services, 177-179, 181-182
    reference staff, 177-180, 182
    reference tools, 44-47
    search strategies, 33, 37, 38
fast fact resources *see* Ready reference
Federal Depository Libraries program, 134
gazetteers, 49, 56, 122
geographic resources, 121-124, 136, 144, 153
government documents, 131-155
handbooks, 49, 56, 114, 135-136, 152
index and abstract services, 137, 145
    see also Databases
    see also Periodical indexes
indexes, 46, 56, 68, 72, 114, 122
intergovernmental organizations, 161-162
Internet, 59-62, 64, 159
keywords, 31, 35, 37, 64-65, 68, 136, 141
    see also Search
legal requirements, 29
legislative publications, 138, 145, 149-150, 154-155
library collection as a reference tool, 168
literature searches, 11, 71
manuals, 49, 114, 135
maps, 121, 122, 136, 144
models of reference services, 14-15
news summaries, 114
non-governmental organizations, 162
online chat facilities, 15, 22-23, 24
online resources, 59-69, 83, 98, 167, 171
online searching, 37-38
    see also Search
opinion polls, 165
organizational directories, 92
periodical indexes, 59, 66-68

see also Databases
see also Index and abstract services
physical environment, 3, 10
    see also Reference section
Publishing and Depository Services, 140, 141
reader education, 11
Readers' Advisory, 10, 22, 165-167
ready reference, 10, 49, 113, 114, 115, 135
    queries, 56, 169
    tools, 49, 115, 135, 136
    uses of, 49, 113
Reference collection, 10, 43, 168, 177
    see also Reference section
reference interview, 19-26
reference section, 3, 6, 10, 179
    see also Reference collection
reference services, 9-17
    access to, 3, 23-24
reference staff, 4-5, 178
reference tools, 43-58
    acquisition of, 10, 177
    characteristics of, 43
    evaluation of, 44-47
    examination of, 47
    sources of, 43-44
    see also Ready reference
reference work, 1-7

referrals, 25
search
    engines, 35, 37, 64-65
    functions, 35-37
    implementation, 35
    strategy, 31-41
    tips, 37, 38, 41
    see also Keywords
    see also Online searching
standards, 159, 160, 161-162
statistics
    as reference tools, 135, 142-143, 152, 165
    of reference transactions, 179
SuDocs classification, 131-134
telephone reference, 23-24
trade directories, 107-108
travel guides, 122, 123
United Nations agencies, 158-160
United Nations documents, 157-158
United States government documents, 131-137
URLs, 37, 59-60
virtual reference, 22-23, 24-25
Who's Who, 98-99, 100
Wikipedia, 83
yearbooks, 49, 56, 114-115, 143, 152

LEARN LIBRARY SKILLS SERIES

This series of paperback workbooks introduces skills needed by library science students and library technicians, as well as librarians seeking refresher materials or study guides for in-service training classes. Each book teaches essential professional skills in a step-by-step process, accompanied by numerous practical examples, exercises and quizzes to reinforce learning, and an appropriate glossary.

Learn About Information
International Edition ©2015
Helen Rowe
ISBN: 9781590954331 Paperback

Learn Basic Library Skills
International Edition ©2015
Helen Rowe and Trina Grover
ISBN: 9781590954348 Paperback

Learn Cataloging the RDA Way
International Edition ©2015
Lynn Farkas and Helen Rowe
ISBN: 9781590954355 Paperback

Learn Dewey Decimal Classification (Edition 23)
International Edition ©2015
Lynn Farkas
ISBN: **9781590954362** Paperback

Learn Management Skills for Libraries and Information Agencies
International Edition ©2015
Bob Pymm
ISBN: 9781590954379 Paperback

Learn Library of Congress Classification
International Edition ©2017
Lynn Farkas
ISBN: 9781590954386 Paperback

Learn Library of Congress Subject Access
International Edition ©2016
Lynn Farkas
ISBN 9781590954393 Paperback

Learn Reference Work
International Edition ©2016
Lynn Farkas and Helen Rowe
ISBN: 9781590954416 Paperback

LIBRARY SCIENCE TITLES

LibrarySpeak:
A Glossary of Terms in Librarianship and Information Technology,
International Edition ©2015
Lynn Farkas
ISBN: 9781590954423 Paperback

My Mentoring Diary:
A Resource for the Library and Information Professions
Revised Edition ©2015
Ann Ritchie and Paul Genoni
ISBN: 9781590954430 Paperback

TOTALRECALL PUBLICATIONS, INC.
1103 Middlecreek,
Friendswood, TX 77546-5448

Phone: (281) 992-3131
email: Sales@TotalRecallPress.com
Online: www.totalrecallpress.com

www.ingramcontent.com/pod-product-compliance
Lightning Source LLC
Chambersburg PA
CBHW080026080526
44586CB00017B/2139